The Best For Last

A Naturalist Settles in Santa Barbara

By

Phila Rogers

Published by the Santa Barbara Company

www.philarogers.com

Nature's Note reprinted from Sam News, the monthly publication
of the Samarkand Retirement Community

Cover Painting by Karin Shelton

Design and Production by Judit Muller

First Printing

ISBN: 978-0-578-52019-3

For my
California Family,
North and South

Contents

Essays

Nature's Note

Nature's Note is the monthly column for *Sam News*, the publication of the Samarkand Retirement Community.

A Life Considered

Five years ago, I moved to Santa Barbara. With my house sold in Berkeley where I'd lived for 63 years, there was no turning back. I think Santa Barbara was inevitable. I grew up with the stories my parents told me of growing up in what was then a small town of 10,000. They had both come out from Wisconsin as small children in the early 1900s, brought by parents who were, no doubt, weary of the harsh winters. Fashioning myself as a 'tomboy,' I especially relished hearing about how dad and his buddies built a shack up San Roque Canyon, and I have sketchy recollections of an expedition to Santa Cruz Island to shoot wild boar. My mother, raised by a chilly, Victorian mother, led a more circumscribed life. A picture shows her as a young girl in the old Mission garden which she told me was her sanctuary.

My parents both came north to college, my mother to Stanford and my father to UC Berkeley. When his father died, leaving a sister and mother alone, he felt he needed to be making a living. After being married in my mother's family home, they returned to Berkeley, and after I was born to a house in the Oakland hills.

After my sister was born, an attic bedroom was built for me which became my sanctuary. I relished the small view to the distant hills and the way rain pounded on the roof. With trees to climb and a creek nearby in a shaded canyon, I developed such a strong sense of place that I was never truly comfortable anywhere else.

It was that same devotion to a landscape with its familiar sounds, smells and local birds, that as a young married woman, I took with me when I moved to the Berkeley Hills.

My dad and his dad, in the hills above Santa Barbara

My mother as a girl in the Old Mission garden

Later as a widow, with two of my three children now living in Santa Barbara, I experimented living here, but my beloved home in those familiar hills always drew me back. But with an aging house and an aging body which led to the inevitable fall, my family prevailed upon me to move to Santa Barbara. They were right, of course, but it wasn't easy, especially trading what I thought of as an independent life for a communal life in a retirement community in an unfamiliar environment.

By writing about the natural world, I have made Santa Barbara my new place. Now that I'm nearing 90-years-old, my mind though contracting in certain ways has expanded in others. Through reading about other elderly people. especially those sensitive to nature, I find I am not alone.

On my table, I have a stack of library books. The titles include "Somewhere Towards the End," "Bird Cloud," "Dawn Light," "Personal Geography." Closer at hand is my worn copy of an anthology of literature on growing old, titled: 'Songs of Experience" which includes poems, selections from memoirs, diaries, and articles. I have often joked about becoming a rocking chair bird watcher. I think often about how with my diminishing resources, such as energy, I can still avail myself of what nourishes me most.

I'm interested in the thoughts of women in their final years. Right now, I'm reading "Personal Geography: Almost An Autobiography," by Elizabeth Coatsworth. One of her late poems:

Through the windy night something
is coming up the path
towards the house.
I have always hated to wait for things.
I think I will go and meet whatever it is

Now widowed, she writes: "Outwardly I am eighty-three years old, but inwardly I am every age, embodying the emotions and experiences of every period of my growth. She writes that in her armchair, she still travels, saying "the best are ones I have never set foot on .. the empty country back of India, beyond Mongolia, or Greenland with its ruins of Viking homesteads. I do not wish to see them. They swim in my fancy...they are a living part of my thought."

I enlarge my life by imagining trails I have walked in the Berkeley Hills, not with longing, but with the pleasure of revisiting them. I revisit Yosemite and the High Sierra. I have my fears and am often disturbed by troubling dreams. But I sometimes have, brief unbidden moments of pure joy, never knowing the origin. The feeling is quite enough. Happiness most often comes in small tableaus – the way the light shines on a leaf, not in some grand panorama.

I am reading excepts from Bernard Berenson's late life dairy where he continues to appreciate beauty and a zest for life into his nineties. He wonders why he clings to life so tenaciously even with his failing body. "Partly out of mere animal instinct. Partly out of curiosity about tomorrow and the day after tomorrow ... I am still eager to achieve, if only as inspirer".

It's often said that as the body fails, awareness and appreciation of nature becomes more intense. My body is mostly intact though I'm unsteady and am well-advised to look at the ground in front of me to avoid a fall. I tire easily. I love 'creature comforts' like the feel of warmth on my shoulders as a cloud slips away from the face of the sun, or lying on something comfortable looking at the sky and at the different ways leaves move in the breeze.

Being a sensual creature, the word 'savor' comes to mind when I want to describe my attachment and response to nature. Fragrance, for instance. Though my sense of smell is somewhat distorted I remember how the sweet peas really smell as I pick them. The sages in the garden ring true, which is why I love them.

But I think I savor wind above all. I love the way it lifts my hair and blows into my nostrils, revitalizing me. I love its signature in the long grass. The way it soughs in the pines, rustles the oak leaves, roars in the eucalyptus, and swishes in the palms. I like to think the wind brings me messages from far away, or carries the essences of me far off to some place I will never see.

Today is a gray morning with coastal fog subduing color and hiding the mountains from view. But by noon, the sun should burn through, color will return, and most likely an afternoon breeze will set my small world into motion. I'll set down my book and step outside.

JUNE 26, 2014

Making It Work on the South Coast

I don't think I could have written these words even two months ago because I was still unreconciled to my move to Santa Barbara. "This is NOT my home," I would have told you. And then I would begin my rant. "Where are the robins to sing up the dawn? Where are the chickadees chattering in the oaks, or the Great-horned Owls hooting at dusk from the eucalyptus?"

Nothing was right. Here, it's a cacophony of crows — an unholy chorus — from dawn to dusk. The creek next to this retirement "campus" is dry as a bone, lacking the lush streamside vegetation to attract the spring singers like the Swainson's Thrushes, Warbling Vireos, and Wilson's Warblers that populated my beloved Strawberry Canyon.

Some days, I would imagine sitting on the bench under the sheltering branches of the oak I had planted 60 years ago. Or I would envision myself at the UC Botanical Garden, climbing the path up to the Old Roses garden, and to the fence line where I could look up the steep, chaparral-covered slope to the bent tree at the top of the hill. Coming down, I would stop to view the Bay in the "V" of the hills. Of course, there would be robins singing everywhere, and the Olive-sided Flycatcher calling from its perch at the top of a redwood.

American Crow

BOB LEWIS

There's no cure for this nostalgia other than to acknowledge that I may always look at what's around me through Berkeley eyes. I don't want to surrender that perspective. But maybe I could allow myself to consider the virtues of the South Coast of Santa Barbara where everyone wants to come and visit and — if they could afford to — stay.

Yellow-rumped Warbler

A month after I came to live here last September, flocks of Yellow-rumped Warblers arrived, just like the ones in Berkeley. The manicured gardens of lawns, palms, and agapanthus beds were just fine with them. They dove into the palms and out again, forever "chipping." Then a Hermit Thrush took up winter residency beneath the live oaks below my bedroom window. And then a troupe of cheerful White-crowned Sparrows arrived, singing sweetly, but in an unfamiliar dialect.

My retirement community is just up the hill from Oak Park, one of the scruffier city parks but with some fine live oaks and sycamores. Sycamores are new to me except for the ones I would infrequently see inland where they favored the flats near streams. They are the true eccentrics in the plant world — no two trees alike. Gravity often has its way with them, pulling long branches in deep curves that almost

White-crowned Sparrow

Tiger Swallowtail

reach the ground, while other limbs look to the sky and grow upward in search of the sun. The trunks near the ground are often covered with thick, brown bark that gives way to thin plates of bark that continually shed, revealing patches of pale brown, gray, olive, and bright russet in newly exposed areas. I am always reminded of a pinto pony. The upper limbs — rising high above the somber live oaks — are almost pure white, especially stunning against a blue sky.

Sycamores are attractive to birds partly for the opportunities they provide the cavity nesters. The larger holes invite woodpeckers and owls, with the smaller holes attracting house wrens, nuthatches, bluebirds, and many others. Certain species of hummingbirds gather the down under the leaves to line their nest,

Western Sycamore

while those winged beauties, the tiger swallowtail butterflies, leave behind eggs which become the voracious caterpillars that find the big palmate sycamore leaves to their liking.

Mission Creek, considered the only perennial stream in the area, borders the park. But this part of the creek, a mile or so from where it enters the ocean, is always dry this time of the year. Only once during this record dry winter did a good rain fill Mission Creek with a wild white-and-tan froth of racing water. From its bank, I could hear the torrent rearranging rocks in the creek bed. The next day, the flow had slowed to a few reflective pools connected by a trickle of running water. One day later, the water had disappeared — gone! And it's been dry ever since.

I walk down the hill to the park most days, crossing a bridge where I often stop to examine the placard describing how the creek bed has been restored by removing tons of concrete that had acted as a barrier to the passage of the endangered Southern

PHILA ROGERS

Descriptive placard on Tallant Road bridge

Steelhead Trout. In better times, the fish might have entered the creek from the ocean during winter storms, ascending the creek to spawn in the upper watershed where water remains year round. But not this year. Even the upper watershed in the Botanic Garden has been reduced to a few stagnating pools, with only the thinnest trickle of water in certain places.

Sometimes I drive up into the foothills to visit the Botanic Garden, which like the one in Tilden Park, Berkeley is devoted exclusively to plants native to California. The upper part of the canyon has its share of live oaks, small bays, and towering sycamores, but none of the dense riparian vegetation to attract the streamside breeders that fill Berkeley's Strawberry Canyon with their joyous songs.

Many of the birds in the South Coast canyons are the ones you might expect to see inland in the Bay Area — Acorn Woodpeckers, White-breasted Nuthatches (instead of Red-breasted), Phainopeplas, sometimes Canyon Wrens, and Wood Pewees. Stellar's Jays are seldom seen in the lower elevations. Swainson's Thrushes pass through in migration, only breeding in the rare streamside where the vegetation conceals this shy bird that mostly reveals its presence through its song.

Today I visited such a place — Atascadero Creek in nearby Goleta, which is tidal below its check dam. But above the dam, its fresh water section supports a jungle of willows, cottonwoods, a few small live oaks, and the first Big-leafed Maple I've seen since coming south. I heard two singing Swainson's Thrushes, several Wilson's Warblers, and a singing Black-headed Grosbeak with a begging juvenile.

Here at the Samarkand, House Finches continue to build nests on any flat surface and the Lesser Goldfinches empty my feeder in a day. But the Orange-crowned Warblers, who sang until a week ago in the park, have ceased singing, confirming that the summer doldrums will soon be upon

Acorn Woodpecker

us with few surprises in the bird world, along with the uninspiring sequence of daily fog and sun.

Time to look to the local beaches, where shorebirds are beginning to migrate along the coast. Shorebirds, mostly gray or brown during the winter, are my weak link. With my Sibley bird book open, I'm trying to bone up on leg length and color, beak differences, and feeding habits. Best idea is to find a walking companion more knowledgeable than I.

Arriving at Samarkand from Berkeley

The Other Side of the Mountain

Fom my bedroom windows, I look up at the rocky wall of the Santa Ynez Mountains. The mountains rise twice as high as the Berkeley Hills, so much higher than I'm used to that I'm always startled when I see them. While the Berkeley Hills are dense with houses and green with planted trees, the Santa Ynez are mostly stony ramparts with thin patches of gray-green chaparral.

The only way to penetrate the mountains is through the narrow canyons carved out over time by running water. Even then, the going is rough, requiring boulder hopping and at times squeezing through almost impenetrable thickets.

The mountains do have their gentler moments when the chaparral blooms briefly white in February and then pale blue in April. Sometimes in the winter the rocky face is laced with waterfalls which disappear in a day.

Late in the day when the low sun slants across the mountain face, shadows fill the canyons and the mountains look soft and approachable. At sunset, the mountains have their finest moment when the alpenglow suffuses the peaks with orange-gold as if the mountains were being heated from within.

The rest of the time, the south-facing mountains, under the unrelenting sun, look harsh and forbidding. For relief, my eyes invariably trace the high ridge where a broken line of green conifers look like miniature cones from the distance. I

PHILA ROGERS

The Santa Ynez Mountains from my window at Samarkand. Coulter pines just visible on ridgeline.

Coulter Pine

learned that the drought-tolerant Coulter Pines produce monster cones weighing up to eight pounds (maybe the largest in the world) while the trees hang on to their anchorage in such an inhospitable place.

Since coming to Santa Barbara almost nine months ago, I have been eager to see them up close. My grandson was game for the trip, so last week on a bright sunny morning we drove up San Marcos Pass (highway 154 on the road map).

In ten minutes we were at the right turn to East Camino Cielo. The narrow, but paved road, passes first through a dense, shady grove of madrone and tanoak trees like the groves I had last seen at Mount Tamalpais, in Marin County. I learned that this was, indeed, the southern-most outpost for these species.

Growing dark and ragged on the steep, north-facing slope — could these trees be Big-coned Spruce? If so, this may be the northern limits for this tree, so familiar to those who frequent the mountains of Southern California.

Coulter Pine cones (among the biggest and heaviest in the world)

Big-cone Spruce. Photo courtesy of Santa Barbara Botanic Garden

This transverse mountain range running east to west contrary to most of the coastal mountains, is truly a "Hadrian's Wall" a kind of "don't cross" line separating certain Northern California flora from Southern California flora. Those plants requiring more moisture can make it on the lee-side of the ridge where fog drip and heavier rainfall meet their needs.

Absorbed as I am by my immediate surroundings, I remember to look up to take in the superlative views — north to the higher inland ranges like the San Raphaels and then south over the Channel, half-lost in the summer haze. I could just make out the slumberous profile of Santa Cruz Island on the horizon. Most arresting of all was the view down into the drainage of the Santa Ynez River where steeply-sloping hills are so dry and thin-soiled that almost nothing can grow there. I wonder if even abundant winter rains could touch them with green.

Closer at hand were other surprises. What's this? A small cottonwood with shining leaves vibrating in the breeze?. Cottonwoods belong near water. What is it doing in these sere mountains? Maybe the crease where it was growing is a moist seep hidden from view.

A few plants are still blooming — the golden-petaled monkey flower, the red blooms of the hummingbird sage. Manzanitas which had bloomed in late winter now bear the round green fruits whose Spanish name means little apples.

And more surprises — sword ferns in the shadiest, most protected places. Scattered about are young big-leaved maples, another moisture lover, which brings a touch of gold to the fall landscape.

The air was both fresh and still, the silence profound, with only a calling Wrentit to disturb the silence. How divine it would be to camp here, to see the wheeling constellations and to watch a sunrise. But the nearest campground is some miles away down along Paradise Road which

View north toward the San Raphael Mountains

BOB LEWIS

Wrentit

parallels the river, but with none of the vistas offered by this highest ridge of the Santa Ynez Mountains.

I am thinking of my father as a boy, in the framed, black and white photograph of him and his dad which hangs in my daughter's office. He is a lad, perhaps twelve years old, and like his father holds a rifle at his side. Wearing a slouch hat with his trousers tucked into his high laced boots, he looks utterly happy to be out on a trail in these same mountains. A boy and his dad with their guns. I neglected to ask him before he died whether he sometimes saw condors riding the thermals over the back country mountains.

Half of me still lives in my memories of Northern California where the hills and mountains are so different. Instead of sharp, irregular profiles against the sky with their "bones" revealed, "my" hills and mountains are curvaceous, voluptuous, plump, and most often further softened

by a covering of grass. Where a hill curves inward, toward its neighbor, the seams are filled with dark green live oaks and bays.

My daughter, when visiting Berkeley, would always notice the cool, blue light, and mention the rumble of the cities below. I often felt caught between her love of Santa Barbara, and my father's preference for "the brisk, invigorating Bay breezes" which seemed to energize him. He was not a fan of laid-back Santa Barbara and its soft, silken air. He rarely returned, and I sensed always with reluctance. I sometimes wonder what he would think, knowing that his fellow, nature-loving daughter had forsaken the vigor of the Bay Area, for this somnolent place.

Back in Santa Barbara in time for lunch, it required effort to reorient myself, even after only two compressed hours in such a high, wild place. I plan on returning often, heartened by how close I am to wilderness.

The Way It Was

Sitting on a bench at Franceschi Park in the foothills above Santa Barbara, I look out over the city. The streets are laid out in grids, dense with houses and buildings. The beach is backed by rows of tall palms. The harbor is filled with boats of every description. I can't help but think about how the same scene would have looked a few hundred years ago.

Wiping the palette clean, what I now see is a narrow plateau sloping gradually to the sea. The conical, thatched huts of a Chumash village cluster where a stream enters the ocean. Offshore are several plank canoes with paddlers headed across the Channel to smaller villages on the Santa Cruz and Santa Rosa Islands.

This scene persisted until the arrival of Europeans in the late 1700s, when the Spanish coming up from Mexico established a string of missions along the coast. At the larger missions, such as the one at Santa Barbara, a small village grew up around its presidio.

It was to this Santa Barbara on a warm and windless January day in 1834, that The *Pilgrim*, a brig out of Boston, dropped

THE PILGRIM
from an oil painting in the possession of Mrs. J. M. Williamson

The Pilgrim

anchor offshore. Aboard was a young student from Harvard, Richard Henry Dana. He would later write the story of his adventures on the high seas and along the coast of California for a year of gathering hides and tallow. His story would become one of best-loved books of American literature: "Two Years Before the Mast."

What Dana saw at Santa Barbara was a small village of about 100 white-washed adobes with red-tiled roofs, surrounding the larger presidio. The mission built on a slope above the town served as a landmark when the vessels came to drop anchor.

"The town is finely situated with a bay in front, and an amphitheater of hills behind. The only thing which diminishes its beauty is that the hills have no trees upon them, they having been all burnt by a great fire which swept them off about a dozen years ago, and they have not yet grown again. The fire described to me by an inhabitant, as having been a terrible and magnificent sight. The air of the valley was so heated that the people were obliged to leave the town and take up their quarters for several days upon the beach (January 1835)."

As a lad from Massachusetts, he would have expected the hills and mountains to be covered with trees. He must have been puzzled by the

dry, central California landscape where steep sandstone mountains could only support gray-green chaparral.

Sailing ships coming to Santa Barbara typically anchored three miles offshore, as this was an exposed and dangerous roadstead.

"The whole swell of the Pacific Ocean rolls in here before a southeaster, and breaks with so heavy a surf in the shallow water, that it is highly dangerous to lie near in to the shore during the southeaster season, that is, between the months of November and April. The wind is the bane of the coast of California (January 1835)."

1830s view of the Santa Barbara harbor

1830s view of Santa Barbara

Lassoing cattle

Along the length of the California coast only San Diego and Monterey offered a reasonably safe anchorage, with San Francisco Bay offering the most secure. Dana extols San Francisco Bay, prophesizing that San Francisco will someday be one of the great cities.

The crew of The *Pilgrim* spent almost a year on the California coast gathering and preparing hides for transport back to Boston, where factories produced finished leather goods. Hide and tallow were the principle exports at a time when the land was divided into vast ranchos where herds of long-horned cattle roamed freely.

On one trip up the coast to Point Conception, the ship encountered a ferocious gale that blew unabated for three nights and days. Even some of their reefed sails were ripped, and they were blown far out to sea. Point Conception and Point Arguello, located where the coast bends inward, are still notorious for brutal winds in all seasons.

The *Pilgrim* made several stops at Santa Barbara over the year. One visit was when the youngest daughter of the De La Guerra family married the American agent, Alfred Robinson. It was a grand ceremony beginning at the Mission and continuing with a "fandango," at the De La Guerra hacienda, lasting several days and nights.

Dana described the deterioration of the Missions following Mexico's winning independence from Spain, twenty-one years earlier. Under Mexican rule, the

Fiesta 2016 poster

JEREMY HARPER

Missions were stripped of their power and lands, leaving the Fathers with only religious duties.

Shortly before setting sail for the east coast Dana encountered Thomas Nuttall, the famous British collector of plants and birds (our Oak Park woodpecker, Nuttall's Woodpecker is named for him). He had been most recently botanizing in Califonia and came aboard as a passenger on Dana's present ship, "The Alert," homeward bound for Boston. For Nuttall's eccentric ways, Dana dubbed him "old curiosity."

In 15 years, California became a state, and the Pastoral Era of the great ranchos came to an end. As new people poured into California, the Spanish landholders, unfamiliar with English and lacking cash, were unable to defend their lands against the newcomers. Gold mining would pollute rivers and even San Francisco Bay itself. Giant trees began to fall before the axe, as cities replaced the tiny presidio towns, and grazing lands became farms. Nature itself was transformed with the disappearance of large animals, and with exotic species replacing much of the native vegetation.

*   *   *

THE PERFECT STORM

I have never had the privilege of being a part of a winter storm at sea as Richard Henry Dana did during his winter aboard "The Pilgrim," while off the coast of California in 1864. But I have experienced innumerable storms while living in Coastal California, both north and south. In this driest year in memory, I can't resist reenacting in my mind one such storm.

I'm still living in my house in the Berkeley Hills. It's November. After a few cloudless days, I look up to see cirrus clouds. Formed of ice crystals and blown by high altitude winds into thin wisps, cirrus clouds often precede an approaching storm.

Toward evening the wind begins to pick up out of the south, bringing warmer air. At bedtime, the rain is yet to fall, but the stars have disappeared behind thickening clouds. The building winds bring a palpable tension. The eucalyptus creak and groan, their leathery leaves clattering together sound like falling water. The pines sing and sigh.

I'm awakened during the night by the sound of rain falling against the south-facing windows. The wind blows unabated with harsh gusts rattling the windows in their frames

At daybreak, following a restless sleep, I awake to the rain still falling. The street is littered with streamers of bark and torn leaves. The wind becomes erratic blowing this way and that, releasing a final deluge of rain. And then all is silent and the air grows chilly. Clouds race across the sky allowing brilliant sun to shine through. As the wind shifts to the north, remaining clouds gather into towering cumulus. On the western horizon, they move south like galleons under full sail.

Fragrances are released that I'd forgotten about. Streams flow again. The dry earth is saturated. The wind has curried the trees releasing all that is tired and spent. The revived earth is born anew.

*   *   *

Up and Down California in 1860-1864: The Journal of William H. Brewer

William Brewer's first view of Santa Barbara in 1861 was from the back of a mule. Brewer was part of the California State Geological Survey responsible for conducting a geological and topographic survey of the state, with an eye to identifying mineral resources.

With gold fever having subsided, the new state legislature wanted to have a systematic survey of state's resources. The well-known geologist, Josiah Whitney, headed the survey. William Brewer's title was that of "Principle Assistant, in charge of the Botanical Department." He was responsible for the fieldwork and for keeping detailed records of what was collected, measured, and observed.

With indefatigable energies and an insatiable curiosity, Brewer keep not only the field notes but managed a voluminous correspondence which became the basis for his journal: "Up and Down California in 1860–1864," edited by Francis P. Farquhar and published by the Yale University Press in 1930. My copy, a beautiful edition generously illustrated, was inscribed to my father by Mr. Farquhar. Mr. Farquhar at the time was the editor of the Sierra Club Bulletin and himself a mountaineer and author.

The survey party camping near Mt. Diablo

William Brewer and his party departed from Boston, not on a sailing ship, but on a streamer bound for Panama. They crossed the isthmus by train to board another steamer for San Francisco. Like those before him and those after, he was overwhelmed by the beauty of the Bay and impressed by the substantial look of the young city. Brewer compared the early November day, to the finest Indian summer day on the east coast, "but without the smoke."

From San Francisco, the party steamed south to San Pedro near Los Angeles. After leaving Los Angeles, they traveled north, exploring the coastal terrain, arriving to the Santa Barbara region the end of February.

East of Santa Barbara, Brewer climbed a high ridge alone. He discovered a variety of shells weathered out of the rocks "as thick as any sea beach and in good preservation." He writes:

I cannot describe my feelings on that ridge, that shore of an ancient ocean. How lonely and desolate! How many decades of centuries, have elapsed since these rocks resounded to the roar of breakers, and these animals sported in their foam ... no human being was within miles of me to break the silence. And then I felt overwhelmed with the magnitude of the work ahead of me ... doing field work in this great state, a territory larger than New England and New York, complicated in its geography.

They arrived at the town of Santa Barbara on March 7. The steamer was to leave that night for San Francisco. With only two steamers a month, Brewer comments on Santa Barbara's isolation where only horse trails connected the community to other

The stony face of the Santa Ynez mountains

Shell fossil found in Santa Ynez Mountains, on display at the Santa Barbara Museum of Natural History

settlements to the north. The first, rough wagon road north would be completed later in the spring.

Brewer's observances about the "decadent town" were much like Dana's thirty years earlier.

The mission was founded about the time of the American Revolution — the locality was beautiful, water good and abundant. A fine church and ecclesiastical buildings and a town sprung up around. The slope beneath was all irrigated and under high cultivation — vineyards, gardens, fields, fountains once embellished that lovely slope. Now all is changed. The church is in good preservation, with a monastery along side — all else is ruined.

Old grapevine near Montecito

The first two weeks camping near Santa Barbara were most unpleasant (Brewer uses the word "abominable.") The persistent dense, wet fog meant tramping through wet bushes and thoroughly soaked their campsite.

Brewer describes riding along the beach with two locals, where they observed asphaltum, a kind of coal-tar which oozes out of the rocks and hardens in the sun. "It occurs in immense quantities and will eventually be a source of some considerable wealth." (But it was oil itself underlying the Channel that would be the source of wealth in the next century.)

Once the sun came out again, several of the party rode to the hot springs five miles east and took a refreshing bath in the hot waters, on the way passing "the most remarkable grapevine I have ever seen."

With the return of the sun, Brewer and a companion set out carrying their barometer in its heavy box, climbing the rocky slopes to the highest ridge where the barometer would register the elevation.

Reaching the first peak, we struck back over a transverse ridge, down and up, through dense chaparral, in which we toiled for seven hours. This is vastly more fatiguing than merely climbing steep slopes: it tries every muscle in the body. We reached the summit at an altitude of 3,800 feet above the sea . . .
. . I never before suffered from thirst as I did that day. The moon was bright as we struck down the wild, dangerous trail. Occasionally a snatch of song would awaken the echoes above the clattering of hoofs of the mules over rocks.

Before leaving Santa Barbara, they joined in the celebration of Easter. The festivities of Holy Week, proved more irksome than pleasurable for Brewer as he had to extricate some of his men, who had been jailed for brawling and drinking.

The survey continued its work traversing the state in all directions before returning to Boston in late December 1864.

During his almost four years in California, Brewer experienced back-to-back the wettest and driest years on record. During the winter of 1863, The Central Valley was under water. Crops were destroyed and cattle drowned.

The following year was desperately dry. On May 27, 1864 he writes:

We came on up the San Jose Valley, twenty-one miles. The day was intensely hot, 97 degrees, the air scorching and dusty. The drought is terrible. In this fertile valley there will not be over a quarter crop, and during the past four days' ride we have seen dead cattle by the hundreds. The hot air trembled over the plain,

Sacramento under water in 1863

and occasionally a mirage seemed to promise cool water, only to vanish as we approached.

William Brewer returned to the East Coast and a successful academic career at Yale. He married again and fathered several children after losing his first wife and newborn son, shortly before departing for California.

Though the survey was a disappointment to some as it is doubtful that the results led to immediate economic gain, but much was learned about the mining regions. According to Francis Farquhar in the introduction to the book, " ... great progress was made toward the understanding of the geological history of the country."

* * *

GRASSLANDS

No other plant community speaks more poignantly of the California seasons than the grasslands — emerald green in the winter and early spring and tawny gold in the summer and fall. In the undulating, rippling sea of grass you see the wind's signature. Once, a quarter of the state was covered by grassland. But what I celebrate today is profoundly different from the grasslands before the arrival of the Europeans in the late 18th century.

The native perennial grasses have been mostly replaced by the imported European annuals, like wild oats, whose seeds were often embedded in the fur of the long-horned cattle brought by the first Spaniards and Mexicans. The predominately native perennial grasses were not adapted to the heavy grazing

Spring grasses and bush lupines

pressure. As the native perennials declined, the European annuals moved in. Grasslands, more than any other plant community, were affected by the arrival of the newcomers

The Bear Flag, the flag of the brief-lived republic before California became a state, shows the long-gone grizzly and the native perennial grasses which grew well spaced from one another. Spring wildflowers put on their annual display in these open spaces.

By the time William Brewer and the survey arrived in California the grasslands had been irrevocably altered.

Those interested in restoration have reintroduced bunch grasses in certain areas, finding that redoing is slower business than the original undoing.

*   *   *

As a child, I reveled in grasslands. In the spring I rolled in the grass, staining my clothes green. I loved the pliant blades, and how green grasses held a trace of moisture even on dry days. I was soothed by the grassland simplicity, not yet understanding its complexity, seeing only an undifferentiated sea of blades. I liked that grasses accentuated the curve of the hills rather than hiding the contours under a coarser cover.

In the summer-dry grass, I would search for singing crickets, but they always stopped singing with my approach. The wind hissed in the dry stalks and picked up the seed-bearing fluff of dandelions carrying it off to new places. Dry grass, even though now lifeless, smelled sweet, like barns full of hay.

Before dying back, grasses cast out their seeds. Half buried, the seeds lay dormant, until the first rains in the fall coaxed open the hard seed, liberating the first tiny blades of new grass. During the rainy months of winter, the lengthening grass spread over the hills like a green tide.

*   *   *

For the Love of Birds

Ralph Hoffman begins the introduction to his wonderful bird book, "Birds of The Pacific States," first published in 1927, with a paraphrase from one of Cicero's orations extolling the delights of studying literature and how it enriches life. Hoffman then paraphrasing further, applying Cicero's words to the study of birds:

It (the study of birds) develops keen observation in youth and is a resource in old age, even for the invalid if he can but have a porch or a window for a post of observation. Birds become the companions of our work in the garden and of our walks...

He concludes with:

If a parent wishes to give his children three gifts for the years to come, I should put next to a passion for truth and a sense of humor, love of beauty in any form. Who will deny that birds are a conspicuous manifestation of beauty in nature?

I keep next to me my copy of "Birds of the Pacific States" given to me by my parents in the 1930s. I was smitten with birds, thanks to my Girl Scout troop and the work we did towards our bird badge. From experienced teachers, we learned the birds of the garden, and, on a nearby lake, winter waterfowl. It is no exaggeration to say that my life was transformed forever.

And it may have been inevitable that in my old age I moved from Berkeley to Santa Barbara, Hoffman's home where he wrote my treasured book.

His book has a way of truly experiencing a bird rather than simply identifying it. A simple system of identifying a bird alone would have to wait for Roger Tory

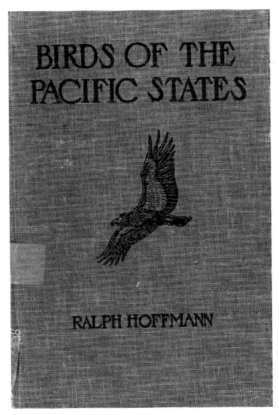

My original copy of "Birds of the Pacific States," by Ralph Hoffman, a gift from my parents in the 1930s

An illustration of a Brown Towhee from Hoffman's "Birds of the Pacific States"

Peterson's *Field Guide to Western Birds*, published first in 1941 (also given to me by my parents) where the salient features of a bird were indicated by arrows. Further description was minimal, stating only that, in the case of a Brown Towhee: "A dull gray-brown with a moderately long tail; suggests a very plain overgrown sparrow."

But read what Hoffman has to say about the Brown (now the renamed California) Towhee, a common bird found in the countryside and in most of our gardens:

Can even a bird-lover become enthusiastic over a Brown Towhee — a plain brown bird that hops stolidly in and out of brush heaps...with no bright colors, no attractive song and no tricks or manners of especial interest? The bird is a rustic with the stolidity of the peasant and apparently lives its entire life near the spot where it was born.

Now there is the "essence" of the towhee!

And how grateful I was that within a week of arriving at my new home in Santa Barbara, I discovered a towhee scratching in the dry leaves.

Inserted into the pages of my copy of Hoffman's book is an article from *Natural History* magazine written by Harold Swanton in 1982 titled "Ralph Hoffman: Unsung Guide to the Birds" subtitled "Early bird guides concentrated on birds in the hand: a New England schoolmaster produced the first for birds in the bush."

The earlier publication in 1904 of Hoffman's a *"Guide to the Birds of New England and Eastern New York"* was considered to be the first true bird guide.

Hoffman from a Natural History *magazine article in 1982*

View of the Channel Islands from Santa Barbara

After teaching Latin is several private schools in the east, Hoffman came west in 1919 to again teach Latin at the Cate School for Boys in Santa Barbara. As a graduate of Harvard and the son of a distinguished Latin and Greek scholar, Ferdinand Hoffman, who ran a boy's school in the East, Hoffman came by the classics naturally.

For the next six years, Hoffman lived in nearby Carpinteria where he had a clear view of the Channel Islands. The islands would draw him across the channel often, first to study birds and later plants. It was at San Miguel Island that he lost his life in a fall from a cliff as he was reaching for a buckwheat.

The Pacific Coast was a new territory for Hoffman and he began almost immediately doing the research which would lead to the publication eight years later of the *Birds of the Pacific States.*

Hoffman's house on Glendessary Lane in Santa Barbara

Swanton writes that "Hoffman had no formal training in ornithology or botany, and although he became an expert in both fields, he retained his amateur status. He brought an amateur's excitement and joy to his work, reflected in every line he wrote."

Hoffman left teaching only when he was given the job as director of the Santa Barbara Museum of Natural History, an ideal job for a man who loved both teaching and the study of natural history.

After the publication of his bird book, Hoffman turned his attention to botany. He took the opportunity on July 21, 1932 to go to San Miguel Island to pursue his study of buckwheat. When he failed to return to the group, after an eight-hour search in heavy fog, his crumpled body was found at the base of an almost vertical cliff. His broken trowel was found next to him. He evidently tried to use his trowel for support.

He is remembered especially at the Museum where a plaque memorializes him. Though now found only through specialty booksellers, *Birds of the Pacific States* remained in print for 50 years.

Joan Lentz, a Santa Barbara birder and author, agrees that Hoffman's *Birds of the Pacific States* is one of the finest field guides every written.

For every lover of birds and nature, his book is an essential part of one's library.

Summer Skies

Santa Barbara natives know that the early summer months are usually the foggiest months of the year. May fog is often referred to as "May Gray" while June is commonly called "June Gloom." Meteorologists refer to fog as stratus. Stratus is defined as a type of low-level cloud, characterized by horizontal layering with a uniform base. I think of stratus simply as a gray lid over the sky.

Though foggy mornings subdue color and are not as cheerful as the days that begin with sunshine, they bring the gift of moisture.

The Coulter Pines, which cling to the rocks along the highest ridges of our mountains, persist because on foggy days their needles comb out moisture, and the accumulated droplets fall like gentle rain. Rain gauges placed under the eucalyptus growing along the ridge tops in the Berkeley Hills collected 10 inches — almost half of the normal yearly rainfall. Under trees, green grass can persist through the summer while grasses in the open turn brown in May.

We welcome the fog especially during the last few years of drought. Everywhere

St. Anthony and the Santa Barbara Mission in the fog

PHILA ROGERS

Altocumulus — a mid-level cloud

bird numbers are down. Species that nest along streams are deprived of water. Some sycamores have turned yellow as if by mimicking fall, rains will come early. The live oaks had no flush of new green leaves this spring. Many of the pines on the upper slopes of Figueroa Mountain have died. Trees weakened by the drought lose their resistance to insect and fungus invasions.

Do we need to be reminded that water is nature's lifeblood?

I spend an inordinate amount of time looking at the sky because I see the sky as a landscape of infinite variety.

Among the most beguiling clouds are the high cirrus clouds, formed of ice crystals and shaped by the high elevation winds into swirls and curls. Sometimes cirrus clouds harbor small rainbows called "sundogs." In the winter, cirrus clouds are often the leading edge of a storm moving down the coast. This time of year, they may indicate southern moisture from the monsoon weather forming over the deserts, or the remnants of a hurricane off the coast of Mexico. In early June what was left of Hurricane Blanca sent us an inch

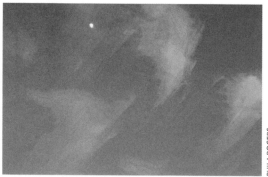

Cirrus clouds at sunset with moon

Summer cumulus above Montecito Peak

PHILA ROGERS

of rain, enough for Mission Creek to flow again briefly.

What excites me most are the summer cumulus which in the afternoon rise above our Santa Ynez Mountains. Once I thought the front range was responsible for the cumulus and I hoped for a possible shower or at the very least a rumble of thunder.

Cumulonimbus, an active thunder head

Since, I've discovered they float above the higher San Raphael Mountains to the north.

For rain, we would need the cumulonimbus, giant heaps of clouds that rise to near 40,000 feet, often with their tops blown off by the high elevation winds. Moving slowly across the landscape, dark streamers of rain trail from their flat bottoms. Cumulonimbus are the most energetic of clouds, containing within columns of rising and falling air, with water

vapor forming around particles which coalesce into rains drops — or in the most extreme form, they can spawn tornadoes.

By late afternoon in Santa Barbara, the heaps of fair-weather cumulus begin to collapse as the sun lowers toward the horizon. During the day, updrafts rising from the sun-warmed earth fed the

Foggy sunset at East Beach.

JOHN NOTEHELFER

cumulus. In the evening, fog begins to move onshore.

Recently, I moved into a different apartment in this retirement community. It suits me in every way. With corner windows facing both south and east, when winter storms finally arrive, the brunt of the rain and wind will fall first against my windows.

From my apartment I can look directly down into the canopy of live oaks and sycamores in Oak Park next door, and up into the successively higher ranges of mountains. When Mission Creek once again has water, I will hear it murmuring over its pebbles in its race to the ocean.

An abundance of sky has given me a chance to learn the flight patterns of various birds. Jays and woodpeckers tend to arrow directly down into the trees. Finches, undulating across the sky, often continue singing even in flight. Crows with

Yellow Warbler

their strong black wings with the ragged tips most often fly in groups. Sometimes they crowd together in the tallest trees setting up fearful cacophony of caws, the braver ones leave the gang to swoop down into lower trees in their attempt to drive off the intruder — most often a hawk or owl.

Crows are ingenious nest builders often including chunks of insulation from a building site, or even pieces of fabric pulled off car covers. They are particularly busy on Mondays, scavenging leftovers from weekend picnics in Oak Park.

Many year-round species like the finches continue to have multiple broods well into the summer. The Lesser Goldfinches are the most interesting to look at as they come in a variety of green and gold — the males with a black cap, dark greenish backs and bright yellow breasts. Some years we may have a breeding pair of the big, flamboyant Hooded Orioles who make clumsy attempts to sip syrup from a hummingbird feeder. The males are deep yellow with a black face and bill and black and white wings. These orioles are never found far from palm trees where they often fasten their beautifully woven, basket-like nest beneath a frond. The nests are sometimes strengthened by the addition to the mix of strong palm fibers.

My favorite summer bird is the Yellow Warbler. Where a stream is available they may select a willow as a site for building a nest, otherwise the proximity of a fountain or a bird bath may do. Their song is as bright as their plumage and is delivered in sweet bursts of melody.

The nest is an open cup, often easily seen, and is the favorite target for the Brown-headed Cowbird. The Cowbird has never developed domestic abilities of their own. Historically, they were always on the move as they followed the bison herds, seizing insects from beneath their hoofs or plucking insects from the animal's fur. They skulk through trees in search of the nests of smaller birds where they lay their egg — producing an egg a day or up

Sparrow removes larger Cowbird's egg from its nest

ROGER BRADFIELD

to 70 in a season. The outcome can be an unhappy one for the host bird, as the cowbird usually hatches first and because of its size and vigor will seize food first from the adult. In the spring, you may see a harried-looking sparrow-sized bird being followed by a bigger, begging cowbird fledgling. Known to parasitism 220 species, no wonder some of the smaller birds have been reduced to an "endangered" status.

But some birds have learned to recognize the cowbird's egg and will either crack the shell or roll the egg out of the nest. Our Yellow Warbler has another strategy. Discovering the cowbird's egg, it will build another nest floor covering the offending egg and lay a new clutch on top. One persistent warbler had to build six new floors before the cowbird gave up!

*   *   *

THE NAMER OF CLOUDS

Luke Howard

A 19th century "citizen scientist," named Luke Howard was the man responsible for the nomenclature of the clouds — terms we still use today. His names were based on Latin (example: cumulus in Latin is "heaps" or cirrus "a curl of hair.") Though a successful London manufacturing chemist, his heart was in the clouds.

He began by naming the three main cloud types — status, cirrus, and cumulus and the intermediate types such as cirro-cumulus and coining the word nimbus which he called the rain cloud.

Cumulus with anvil

LUKE HOWARD

He also published *The Climate of London*, the first book on urban climatology, and another publication on the cycle of 18 years in the seasons of Britain.

Howard's love of clouds and weather began in childhood and never diminished. For his studies he was elected as a Fellow of the Royal Society in 1821.

NOVEMBER 8, 2015

The Elfin Forest — California's Chaparral

For most people, forest means stands of pines and firs or at least deciduous trees like maples, beech and possibly aspen. Entering The Los Padres National Forest, just above Santa Barbara, what do you see? Steep slopes clothed with brush we call chaparral.

Chaparral is the name for that tough assemblage of mostly head-high drought-tolerant, evergreen shrubs that grow where heat and dryness is even too much for grasslands, and the soils are too thin for "real" forest. Chaparral plants are superbly adapted to our region of cool, moist winters and long, hot, dry summers.

Growth and blooming occur at the end of the wet season, in early spring. Once the rains end and the heat increases, chaparral plants shut down. Tough, usually small leaves resist the desiccating sun, while roots reach ever deeper into the sandstone in search of remaining moisture.

You might call chaparral the quintessential California plant, appearing the length of the state from the Oregon border to a short distance into Mexico. Chaparral finds its most perfect expression in the mountains of Southern California where chaparral often extends from horizon to horizon.

STEVE JANUK

Chaparral-covered slopes with white-blooming ceonothus in the foreground. Photo courtesy of the Santa Barbara Botanic Garden

PHILA ROGERS

Toyon berries

Chaparral is associated with the Mediterranean climate which is characterized by short, sometimes wet, mild winters, and a long, often hot summer. Less than three percent of the earth's surface shares this particular climate — most often on the west coast of a continent between 30 to 40 degrees latitude, facing on a cold ocean, with its large high-pressure air mass. The shrubs in each of these regions have their own distinctive species and go by the names maquis, garrigue, matorral, fynbos, or heath.

The manzanitas are typical of our chaparral plants. To save moisture, they turn their leaves sideways to the punishing sun. Companions are other chaparral plants like toyons, ceonothus, and scrub oak.

To ride through the unyielding and sometimes spiny vegetation in pursuit of wayward cattle, Spanish vaqueros wore leather leggings called chaps, short for chaparro, the Spanish name for scrub oak, thus the name chaparral.

Chaparral plants grow in such close association that their tops are often interwoven, creating dense canopies which protect chaparral-loving animals like the shy Wrentit and certain reptiles from view.

Chaparral and fire have always been closely associated. The recent view had been that chaparral depended on fire for renewal. But now, plant scientists, support the idea that mature chaparral can remain healthy indefinitely. Often near populated areas where fires are frequent enough to burn recovering chaparral, the once beautiful and life-filled plant community, may be replaced by non-native grasses and weeds

Where there are infrequent fires, chaparral plants return healthy and vigorous, covering the charred remains in a few years

CAROL BORNSTEIN

Poppies and lupine bloom after a fire. Photo courtesy of the Santa Barbara Botanic Garden

with new growth. In the meantime, the first spring after a fire brings forth a beautiful display of wild flowers called poetically, "fire followers." Their seeds may have laid dormant for decades, sometimes centuries, waiting for their moment, when the chaparral cover is burned in a fire. Whether it's the heat itself, or possibly certain

California Thrasher

chemicals in the smoke, the seeds awaken and a new cycle begins.

After a fire, brilliant blue and rust-colored Lazuli Buntings arrive to sing from the tallest charred branches, and Lawrence goldfinches salvage unsprouted seed. The Wrentits, Bushtits, and California Thrashers — the species living in mature chaparral — are weak fliers and often perish in the flames.

Some years ago, I remember driving up the San Marcos Pass and amongst the charred skeletons of manzanitas, white morning glories twined. Out of the ashes bloomed annual flowers in a multitude of colors — orange poppies, purple phaecelia, yellow goldfields. As the burned chaparral begins putting on new growth, certain small perennial shrubs like bush lupine appear until finally they, too, were shaded out, and

mature chaparral once again takes over the mountain slopes in all shades of green.

In spite of the tough, droughty appearance of mature chaparral, in early spring comes an explosion of flowers. On the mountainsides above Santa Barbara, the white-flowered ceonothus begins blooming in February, frosting the slopes,

Chaparral covering north slope of the Santa Ynez mountains

followed by another species with purple-blue clouds of flowers, subtly fragrant.

In the late afternoon, I remember approaching the Santa Ynez Mountains from the north. The chaparral-covered mountains looked as if they were covered with a deep purple velvet, with even deeper color in the canyons. But the illusion is dispelled on close approach when you are confronted with a wall of stiff, unyielding vegetation, discouraging further investigation except possibly on hands and knees.

Close to the coast, often growing on the sand dunes, is another assemblage of plants sometimes called "soft chaparral." The preferred name is coastal sage scrub. The plants are smaller, softer, often pungently fragrant and unlike true evergreen chaparral are sometimes deciduous, losing their leaves in the dry summer. It's here you'll find various sages, buckwheats, and California sagebrush. I often bring home a sprig of sagebrush in my pocket to tuck under my pillow.

For a conventional wife and mother who helped with homework and had nourishing meals on the table by 6 pm, I harbored very unconventional thoughts. I was drawn to books by women who lived eccentric lives, often pursuing a passion for the natural world. Lately, I had been rereading the two books by Lester Rowntree who spent nine months of the year traveling the state of California in her old Ford touring car, specially adapted to carry tools and the necessary equipment for preserving

Lester Rowntree

plants and collecting seeds. In the high Sierra, she walked beside her faithful burro who carried her gear.

In the late fall, she returned to her mountainside home south of Carmel where she had built a cabin on a slope, surrounded by her native plant garden, overlooking the sea. Even in somewhat domesticated surroundings, she slept with windows and doors open to encourage visits from the foxes and to listen to the changing tides and the sound of pounding waves on the rocks below.

What Lester Rowntree especially loved was chaparral — that most California of all plant communities — which makes us sisters of sorts.

A GIANT IN AN ELFIN FOREST

Maybe it was thinking of Rowntree that made me put on my boots, sturdiest trousers, gather up field guides and plenty of water. I planned on driving up over the top of the Berkeley Hills and head east for Mount Diablo in the inner coast range of Contra Costa County.

I needed to go inland for hard chaparral like the Manzanita and its companions. My Berkeley Hills are mostly open grasslands

Crawling through the chaparral

with a scattering of soft, but durable shrub called coyote bush. On a few isolated slopes, coyote bush teams up with fragrant sages, and becomes what we call "soft" chaparral, which prefers the moister hills near the ocean.

I was looking for a mature stand of chaparral tall enough for me to crawl under. I had read somewhere that this was the only way to penetrate the thickets. I found a promising hillside, parked my car along the edge of the road, hoping to find my way back after an hour or so. I looked

both ways to be sure no one would witness me dropping to my knees and crawling into the brush.

I found myself in a dim and silent world, out of the wind and the strong sun. The tight interweave of leaves, stems, and twigs made an almost impenetrable roof above. I had no difficulty skirting the leafless lower branches. With no understory plants, I had an almost unrestricted view in all directions. The going was easy. It occurred to me that I needed to surface now and then to determine my location. After pushing up through the tangle of abrasive leaves and punishing stems, I was relieved to see my car on the road below.

Submerging again, I felt more confident. I knew of the unique creatures that live in the chaparral. I'd hoped to see a stripped racer, head held high hurrying about on some secret mission, or a California Thrasher scything through the litter with its long curved bill. It appears that an unexpected presence like myself would be largely ignored. Even a shy bird like a Wrentit might come close, cocking its head to fix me with its yellow eye.

But today, I had the chaparral world to myself. Remembering that I had to retrace my route downhill, I came out at the edge of the chaparral a few yards up the road from my car. My exhilaration had masked my fatigue. Tired, I stretched out on the back seat aware now of rich, redolent smell of wild plants clinging to my clothes.

*   *   *

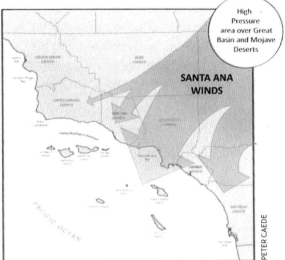

The two diagrams show the different locations of Santa Ana and Sundowner wind in our region. ("A Naturalist's Guide to the Santa Barbara Region" by Joan Easton Lentz)

TWO "CHAPARRAL WINDS"

Sundowners are described as warm downslope winds that periodically occur along a short segment of the Southern California coast in the vicinity of Santa Barbara. Their name refers to their typical onset in the late afternoon or early evening, though they can occur at any time of the day. In extreme cases, winds can be of gale force or higher, and temperatures over the coastal plain and even the coast itself can rise significantly above 100 degrees F.

The more famous Santa Ana winds are a minor player in Santa Barbara. The Santa Anas affect the regions to the south — the Santa Clara River Valley and the Los Angeles basin. Santa Anas form further inland over the Great Basin or the Mojave Desert, taking on the quality of that dry landscape. Under certain conditions, the dry air rushes through the passes of the Southern California mountains, the wind compresses and becomes hotter and drier as it descends.

Sundowners typically originate in the Santa Ynez Valley north of Santa Barbara where the heated air rising in the afternoon or early evening is pent up behind the Santa Ynez Mountains before rushing through the mountain passes toward the coast.

* * *

A SUNDOWNER

I experienced a sundowner last November when I was spending the evening at my family's house in Mission Canyon. It was mild enough to sit outside with a light sweater. The air was calm and sweet smelling from the blooming citrus. Without warning, a violent gust of wind swept down upon us releasing a cascade of leaves from the tree above, slamming doors, and rising a swirl of dust from the path. And then another gust followed, and we scrambled to right the furniture before fleeing inside. The unrelenting, wrenching wind seemed to come from all directions. I was agitated, and dry mouthed. In less than an hour, the temperature went up 20 degrees.

The lights went out as we lost our power. What can be disconcerting when the lights are on, is terrifying in the dark. A thud on the roof told us a frond had no doubt been blown loose from a palm tree.

With no lights, and too dangerous to venture outside, we went to bed. Falling into a restless sleep, I woke up suddenly around 3:00 a.m. to silence. I waited for the next gust of wind, but none came. Even with doors and windows closed I could sense the air was now cool and moist, telling me that our normal onshore flow was back.

I knew daybreak would reveal what the wind had blown down. Even faced with a monumental cleanup ahead, we had escaped fire, which can be a companion of these sundowners.

* * *

Each Santa Barbara season has it own wind. In the winter, Pacific storms approaching the coast are carried on the south winds, sometimes reaching gale force. A passing storm, is most apt to be followed by cool winds from the north or west bringing sparkling clarity.

The prevailing northwest wind in the summer, passing over the colder off-shore waters, often condenses into fog which is drawn inland by rising warm air in the valleys. The fog delivers a valuable gift of moisture. Droplets forming on leaves, drop to the ground like rainfall.

I love the wind. For me it's the breath of life. If I lived in the high prairie of Wyoming where the wind never stops blowing, I would probably feel different. But in temperate Santa Barbara, wind brings the landscape to life. It sets the hillside grasses rippling, trees to murmur and sway, while palm fronds thrash and clatter like a downpour on a tin roof. Without wind or a least a stiff breeze, the air grows stagnant and feels over breathed. Wind brings us our weather as high pressure off the coast rushes toward areas of low pressure.

The Various Forms of Fog

Fog
The fog comes
On little cat feet.
It sits looking
Over harbor and city
On silent haunches
And then moves on

—*Carl Sandburg*

I 've lived in coastal California for all of my 87 years, so you'd think by now I would have developed at least a tolerance for the fog which arrives each summer. But I'm one of those unfortunate people whose moods are dictated by the weather. Awaking to sunshine fills me with good cheer. A gray beginning sets a similar mood for the morning.

Yes, I've heard the arguments — fog delivers at least some moisture in this driest of

Fog over Santa Barbara and up mountain canyons

Beach palms in fog

myself with my library including historical books like "Up and Down California," Brewer's fascinating account of doing a geographic and geological survey of the state in the 1850's, and going a century back to the classical account of California's coast by Richard Henry Dana in "Two Years Before the Mast." I've also been mining Google for gems of information.

Dana didn't mention fog as he was more concerned about the winter when an anchored ship could be caught by a southeast storm gale and be blown ashore before they could set sail for the open ocean.

At the risk of sounding pedantic, here are some basic facts. Our fog — advection fog — comes mostly in the summer months when the Northern Pacific High is in command. That zone of high pressure that squats over the eastern Pacific, fends off storms that might come in from the north, and establishes summer wind patterns. In the late spring and early summer, the wind picks up speed and blows down the coast. The wind displaces the warmer

seasons. And the cloud cover protects plants from desiccation by the summer sun.

I'm also aware that taking the perspective of a naturalist delivers me from being a victim of moods (moods are nice enough when they are cheerful ones). I've spent the last few days doing research, reacquainting

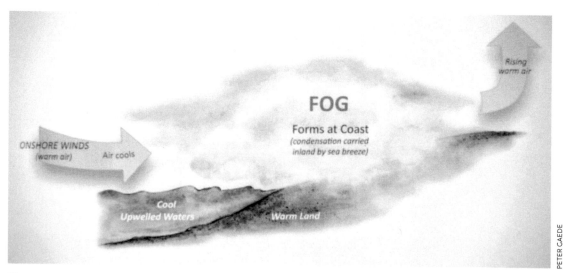

FOG

Forms at Coast
(condensation carried inland by sea breeze)

ONSHORE WINDS
(warm air) Air cools

Rising warm air

Cool Upwelled Waters Warm Land

PETER GAEDE

The movement of fog onshore on a typical summer day ("A Naturalist's Guide to the Santa Barbara Region" by Joan Easton Lentz)

Fog at sunset

surface water causing an upwelling of the deeper, cold water. When the warmer wind passes over the chilly water, the moist air condenses into tiny liquid droplets suspended in the air, forming fog.

Often the fog is drawn inland by the low pressure lying over the hot Great Central Valley. The fog usually retreats back to the immediate coast where it may persist all day, and sometimes for days on end. In Santa Barbara, those foggy days may be called May Gray or June Gloom. In Northern California the winds and chill air at Pt. Reyes makes it one of the foggiest places in the world with an average of 200 foggy days a year.

I favor those late summer and early autumn days of decreasing coastal fogs when the Pacific High begins to slowly shift

Fog drifting through redwoods

south allowing for the possibility of an early rain coming down from the north.

Or when humidity sometimes moves north bringing the possibility of a thunderstorm and wonderful cloud effects. Exotic weather heightens one's senses.

I'm also reading about how coastal fogs along the north coast have allowed the redwood forest to persist. Once, when the climate was much wetter, redwoods were common over much of the continent. But as the climate became drier and cooler, the redwood forests retreated to a narrow band along the immediate coast of Northern California visited by ocean fogs in the summer.

I once read that sunny California has more fog than any other state when you consider that the coast in the summer is often foggy and in the winter, damp, ground-hugging tule fogs covering the Great Central Valley can blot out the sun for days on end until the next rain storm sweeps the fog away for a time. The so-called radiation fog often follows the rain when the earth is both chilled and damp and the drier air above it condenses, forming fog. I remember once driving across the Sacramento Valley at night and I could see that the fog came up to the cow's belly, leaving its head in the clear.

Back to Santa Barbara: In his journal; "Up and Down California" William Brewer writes on Tuesday, March 12 (1861). "Still foggy and wet. This weather is abominable — now for nearly two weeks we have had foggy, damp weather, tramping through wet bushes, riding in damp, foggy air, burning wet wood to dry ourselves, no sun to dry our damp blankets. I find that it makes some of my joints squeak with rheumatic twinges. Went

out this morning, found it so wet that we had to return to camp".

Five days later on Sunday Evening, March 17, he writes: "We have had a clear hot day, after two week's fog, and have improved the opportunity to dry our blankets and clothes, botanic papers, etc."

I don't recall in my four years of living in Santa Barbara of having a foggy spell in March. What does ring true is the strength of the sun. Even on foggy days, as the fog begins to thin one can feel the heat of the

Summer grass kept green by fog drip off trees

PHILA ROGERS

sun. I remember being warned as a child, that I could be badly sunburned by the sun in a light fog.

In the Bay Area where I lived, researchers measured in the rainless summer the equivalent of 10 inches of rain under the pines and eucalyptus along the ridgeline of the foggy Berkeley Hills. I noticed how on my summer walks in the grasslands, yellow and dry by May, I could count on a circle of fresh green grass within the drip line of each tree. The long narrow leaves of the eucalyptus and the slender pine needles did an especially efficient job of combing out moisture from the drifting fog.

HARVESTING FOG

I'm not sure about this, but it's my impression that the west coast of other continents at our latitudes often have summer coastal fog. In the case of Peru, Chile and Namibia in Africa, these are deserts with little or no rain, and no surface or groundwater. A certain Namibian beetle sleeps with its hindquarters raised and in the morning shifts its position to allow the condensed moisture to run into its mouth for a drink. Incas, living on the barren slopes of the west-facing Andes, after observing that pots under shrubs and small trees filled with fog drip, learned to string up nets made of small mesh which would sift drifting fog.

Why not string a series of nets along Twin Peaks in San Francisco? Unfortunately, such a meager harvest could only supply the needs of a small neighborhood. But there are small villages in the arid west coast of South America and elsewhere, where enough water is collected with fog nets to grow crops, irrigate orchards and have enough left over for personal use.

One such community is Bellavista, a village of 200 people on the dry slopes above Lima, Peru. With almost no rain, no river, or groundwater, the village had to be served by expensive water trucks from Lima.

Conservationists Kai Tiederman and Anna Lummerich, working with a non-profit supported in part by National Geographic, showed the villagers how to construct the fog catchers — nylon mesh stretched between poles. The villagers did the heavy work, carrying sand bags 800 feet up the steep hill to stabilize the poles and to build pools to store the collected water.

Fog catchers

The newly-planted 700 tara trees will be able to eventually collect their own water. Tara trees produce valuable tannin.

Stringing up nets

With the wind blowing the heavy fog through the nets they can now collect 600 gallons a day.

Okay, I'm convinced. Bring on the fog and no more grumbling about gray mornings.

AUGUST 22, 2016

The Pleasure of Canyons

*I'm drawn to canyons with their
cool shade
and generous vegetation,
especially in this dry, mostly
mountainous country
of sun-struck rock.
And so is all life.
Birds and other animals come to
where there is moisture,
abundant food, and places to
raise young.*

**THE VIEW FROM MY APARTMENT
ABOVE OAK PARK**

I look northeast to the Santa Ynez
Mountains. The mountains are a transverse
range, one of several ranges so named
because they trend east and west rather
than the usual north-south trend of most
coastal mountains. The town of Santa
Barbara occupies the narrow alluvial plain
between the ocean and the mountains

The mountains are composed mostly
of pale sandstones often embedded

A Canyon trail

Montecito Peak

Montecito Peak on fire, Oct 29, 2015

with fossil shells from the distant past when the mountains were under a warm sea. Reflecting the low winter sun and protecting the region from the chilling north winds, the mountains have a profound effect on the local climate.

My bedroom window perfectly frames Montecito Peak, the most symmetrical of all the named peaks. At midday, when the mountains are evenly lit, they resemble a jigsaw puzzle of pale rock and mats of olive green chaparral. I look hard to try and distinguish a canyon, but it's when the sun is low in the sky before sunset that the mountains reveal their contours. Purple shadows fill the canyons while ridges and peaks glow in the late light. I learned by studying a map that the deep shadow in the saddle west of Montecito Peak is the top of Cold Spring Canyon.

Most canyons have a stream, usually an ephemeral one which appears only briefly after a rain. Others, like Mission Creek,

are considered perennial, but in fact water persists only in the foothills and mountains. Because of the steepness of the Santa Ynez Mountains, most streams, beginning as springs near the top of the range, may drop four thousand feet from their headwaters in a few miles to where they join the Pacific Ocean.

My plan was to hike several of the canyons so I could write about them with affection and authority. On my first try to the San Ysidro Trail on the almost level Ennisbrook Trail, I fell and cracked my ribs.

I saw two solutions — send my two grandchildren with their stout hearts and strong legs into the canyons where they regularly walk. Or I could narrow my canyon and stream observations to Mission Creek, one of the most accessible of the streams which runs (when it does) through Oak Park just below my apartment. So Mission Canyon it is.

MISSION CANYON AND ITS CREEK

Mission Creek and its canyon have a rich history dating back to the Mission days in the late 1700's when the waters were captured behind a stone dam built with Indian labor in 1803. The water was stored in sandstone reservoirs, just above the mission itself. The water irrigated the sloping garden of fruit trees, vegetables and wheat. When Mexico defeated Spain in 1830, the missions lost their authority and most of the Indian labor. The garden quickly fell into ruin along with many of the adobe buildings.

Like most of the streams which flow down the south slope of the Santa Ynez Mountains, Mission Creek begins as springs near the ridgeline and then emerges as a series of cascades and pools, accessible from the Tunnel Trail.

Following James Wapotich's directions in his weekly "Trail Quest" column in the News-Press, I located where the Tunnel Trail begins along East Camino Cielo Road, just beyond the intersection with Gibraltar Road. The trail is marked by an aging metal sign and three large boulders across the dirt road. The trail — a dirt road — continues just beyond the level section when it becomes a narrow trail dropping steeply down to where Mission Creek begins. The Falls are a popular destination for hikers, most hiking up from Tunnel Trail off Tunnel Road. I've never hiked up far enough to reach the falls so I have to rely on the reports of others and the photos they took.

Tunnel Trail at the top off Camino Cielo

Tunnel Trail sign

Mission Creek falls

AT THE BOTANIC GARDEN

Boulders deposited long ago by a debris flow

PHILA ROGERS

Mission dam built by Indian labor in the early 1800s

PHILA ROGERS

It's in the Garden where most of us become familiar with Mission Creek. Before the present four-year drought, regular releases from the Mission Tunnel (which brings water from Gibraltar Reservoir to Santa Barbara) kept the creek refreshed, so one season seemed like another. Now the stream is mostly small ponds, growing green with algae.

Standing on the uneven stones at the top of the Indian dam is a good place to look up and down the steam and to admire the feat of building the dam with hand labor. Once, the stored water was carried down stone aqueducts to the Mission where it not only provided irrigation and drinking water, but filled the stone basins (still there to see above the Rose Garden) where hides were soaked prior to tanning.

ROCKY NOOK PARK

A couple of blocks above the Mission is a charming county park — known by the locals simply as Rocky Nook. And rocky, indeed. Boulders, scattered generously everywhere, were deposited a thousand years ago by a debris flow that roared down the canyon depositing boulders along the way. A Chumash Indian legend says the boulders are the bone remains of the Indians drowned by the slurry of water and sediments. I felt as if I were photographing family groups. In late May at the beginning of the long dry season, the creek is surprisingly active though its flow will most likely decline as the season advances.

Boulder families

PHILA ROGERS

Alder tree

PHILA ROGERS

AT OAK PARK

Since I moved to Santa Barbara three years ago, a four-year drought has reduced Mission Creek at Oak Park to a mostly dry creek bed. Only after a rain of an inch or more would the creek come to life as a muddy noisy, torrent which finally reaches the sea by curving a path across the beach just south of Stearns Wharf.

Dry Mission Creek

Mission Creek after a rain

Within a day, the creek at Oak Park becomes a series of clear pools joined by rivulets of gurgling water. It is then that I walk slowing along its banks, imagining the water circulating through my veins, refreshing my worn and tired body. And I would then know deep peace. The following day, the creek disappeared leaving behind only drying mud where the pools had been.

The creek bed once again is laid bare and often weed-filled. By late spring, the stream even in the foothills at the Botanic Garden, is often reduced to a few algae-filled pools.

Mission Creek leaves its canyon just below the Garden where it is joined by Rattlesnake Creek. Together they meander several miles across the gently-sloping plain (called by geologists an alluvial fan) to the ocean. Over the years, the creek has flooded the town several times during the rainy winter months.

My father, who as a boy lived between Oak Park and Cottage Hospital, remembers those times when the only high spot in their neighborhood was their garden, where the neighbors came and stood until the flood waters receded. During the floods, the creek waters filtered slowing down through the rock and soil replenishing the groundwater. Today, the creek, in some places contained by concrete sides, seldom floods, so it flows directly into ocean carrying with it pollutants, often closing for a time the surrounding beaches as unsafe for swimming.

Oak Park is not a nature park, it's a people park where neighbors walk their dogs and on weekends, it's crowded. Piñatas are hung from the oak branches, musicians tune their guitars and horns, kids play in noisy swarms, and men sweat over the barbecues. In the winter when the days are short and sometimes rainy, Oak Park returns to a more natural state.

Dad's boyhood home on Castillo Street

Mission Creek Outfall

PHILA ROGERS

Black Skimmer fishing

BOB LEWIS

MISSION CREEK OUTFALL

Most of the year, the creek trapped behind its sand berm from continuing to the ocean, forms a quiet lagoon favored by water and shorebirds, especially during the winter. When the creek is in flood stage, it over tops its berm, and carves a curving course across the sand to the ocean.

LOOKING BACK

My love of canyons goes back to a childhood living in the Oakland Hills. There were no houses across the street because at the bottom of the slope was an electric train, part of the Key System, which ran across the Bay Bridge to San Francisco. The dense slope on the other side of the track was a no man's land until I was old enough to venture further afield. What drew me there was an ethereal bird song, I didn't recognize

ROGER BRADFIELD

Slippery Slope

The slope was too steep to navigate on foot so I slid on my behind through what I would later discover was mostly poison oak. After an almost vertical slope of

BOB LEWIS

Swainson's thrush

53

slippery clay, I found myself at the edge of a creek. And there was my bird, silent now, who fixed me with it's round eye, made even rounder by a circle of white feathers. Late in the spring, the creek was reduced to a series of dark pools, laced together by threads of running water. Water striders skated across the surface while dragonflies darted about occasionally touching the water.

I couldn't stay away from this newly discovered world until a painful rash spread across my body after each foray. I later learned that the creek was called Trestle Glen Creek or Indian Gulch Creek named for the Ohlone villages along its margins. Instead of flowing into the ocean, the creek brought its water to Lake Merritt, a tidal sanctuary with an amazing array of winter water birds, attracting enough attention so it became the first waterfowl sanctuary in the country.

In my twenties, we moved to the Berkeley Hills and my stream became Strawberry Creek. The stream, like so many coastal streams, rose in springs near the top of the Berkeley Hills, flowed through the Botanical Gardens, which I came to love and where I met a dear friend with whom I led monthly bird walks. The garden was paradise and a number of birds thought so, too. In the spring, the bird song was almost overwhelming. Thrushes again, including the dearest of all — the American

Lake Merritt, Oakland

Robin, the Black-headed Grosbeaks, Warbling Vireos — on and on — singing an intoxicating symphony of melodies unlike any other stream canyon I know.

I have also learned a new concept for understanding one's place on the planet by determining one's watershed. Our house was on a slope near the top of the Berkeley Hills where most of the water drained toward Strawberry Creek which I liked to claim as defining my home place.

Since moving to Santa Barbara three years ago, my watershed is unequivocally Mission Creek, as it was for my parents who lived nearby more than a 100 years ago.

NOVEMBER 10, 2016

Fall In Santa Barbara

Take this week — in the middle of October. All day the clouds continued to build up against the mountains. And at bedtime, I heard an unfamiliar sound. Opening the door, I was surprised by rain. Pulling open the window next to my bed, I fell asleep to the comforting sound of rain falling, while breathing in that indescribable fragrance of earth refreshed. The morning that followed was the freshest we've had in this endless season of harsh drought.

By Wednesday, the temperature rose to 95 degrees, the humidity descended into the single digits, the red fire danger flags were posted. By the weekend the scene changed again. I could joyfully proclaim fall as it should be — a sky full of clouds of every shape in shades of gray and white. I've cracked open the door so I can feel the cool breeze and hear the birds as I work on my computer.

Nothing energizes the bird population like a change in the weather, especially when there is the possibility of rain. If you trust forecasts, rain may be moving our way, coming from the north, the most reliable direction.

Being an incurable nostalgic, I remember the first rain of the fall brought up sprouts of green grass on the hills, certain native plants set buds or even bloomed, and the

PHILA ROGERS

birds began singing again. I guessed that maybe they were fooled by day and night equaling in length, the way it did during the spring equinox.

More knowledgeable birdwatchers than I call this "second spring" "Autumnal Recrudescence," a word new to me. Looking the word up, I read that it was most often a medical term meaning the return of an illness after a remission. Or it could mean the recurrence of an unpleasant feeling like doubt.

Naturalist give the word a happier meaning.

The Autumnal Recrudescence of the Amatory Urge

When the birds are cacophonic in the trees and on the verge

Of the fields in mid-October when the cold is like a scourge.

It is not delight in winter that makes feathered voices surge,

But autumnal recrudescence of the amatory urge.

When the frost is on the pumpkin and when leaf and branch diverge,

Birds with hormones reawakened sing a paean, not a dirge.

What's the reason for their warbling? Why on earth this late-year splurge.

—Susan Stiles, copyright December 1973

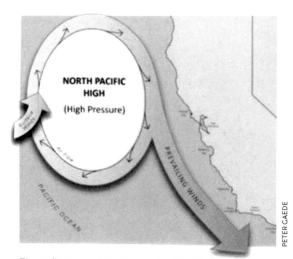

The influence of the North Pacific High Pressure system and its position, shielding the region from low-pressure disturbances from the north in spring and summer. ("A Naturalist's Guide to the Santa Barbara Region" by Joan Easton Lentz)

After the mostly silent late summer, I was delighted with the bird chorus. I also attributed it to the completion of energy-robbing activities like nesting followed by molting where in most species, every feather has to be replaced with a new one.

The arrival of the winter residents certainly energized the local, year-round population. The regulars and newcomers set about declaring and defending their winter territories.

Wanting to better understand fall in Santa Barbara sent me back to Joan Lentz's "A Naturalist's Guide to the Santa Barbara Region," my bible on all things local. She says that the distinction between summer and fall is more pronounced than between spring and summer. Enter our old friend or nemesis The North Pacific High. If the atmosphere behaves as it should, this zone of high pressure which held sway over the summer, producing the northwest winds blowing down the coast and causing coastal fog, should begin to move south following the sun. Winds cease and with them the fog. A rain may even sneak through as it had last Sunday evening. With less fog, the skies are clearer and the blue skies are a palette for the extraordinary clouds of fall.

In the Berkeley Hills where I've lived most of my life, we especially dreaded the August fogs with their frigid winds when the gloomy, damp overcast could persist for days on end. When late September brought relief, we were ecstatic. Both in the Bay Area and in Santa Barbara, fall winds sometimes blew from the north

Liquidambar street trees

and northeast, coming from the Great Basin, bringing the odors of sage and when passing over the mountains, the tangy smell of conifers.

Though Santa Barbara, by its location and topography, is spared the full impact of the Santa Anas (unlike the LA basin), we often have the offshore winds, heat, and lower humidity.

In my drives around town I look for autumn color to further affirm the change of season. Sycamores, which grow wherever there is a little ground moisture, have been dropping leaves all summer and even in the best of years are only a dusky gold, showing their best color when back lit by the sun. Liquidambars, also called sweet gum, a native to the southeast, are beginning to show their autumn color, but we will have to wait until late November for their best display.

Weary of my endless comparisons between Berkeley and Santa Barbara, my daughter decided it was time for a drive over the

mountain to the Santa Ynez Valley, for a change of scene. And change of scene, indeed! What a difference a mountain range makes. The Santa Ynez Valley is hotter in the summer and colder in the winter. The continental influences prevail, moderated somewhat by the proximity to the coast and the ocean. But the sub-tropical trees in Santa Barbara's parks and gardens would not succeed here.

This is the wide-open country of vineyards and olive orchards where the horse is king. Some ranches provide individual horse casitas with white stucco walls, tiled roofs, and individual corrals.

And, yes, I did find the color I was hoping for in the bright yellow cottonwoods growing along the dry Santa Ynez River watercourse. We like to be drenched in the fall brilliance of yellows, oranges, and red — this intoxicating dazzle — the final flaring before the bare trees in the dimming light and short days of winter.

Cottonwoods

But what pleased me the most were the ambers of the vineyards, the pale grasses long spent and all the other shades of gray-greens, ochers, umbers and shades of color for which I have no names — and the swirls and small bunches of white clouds against a soft blue sky.

Once I yearned to live in open country with only distant neighbors if any at all, under a curving sky with stars beyond counting, winds that traveled long distances unobstructed, and the distant yips and howls of coyotes.

But I was content enough to return back over the mountain, to the marine air which is kinder, and to a town of neighborhoods where lights in other windows comfort me. On the weekends, music and voices of children come up the hill from the city park below. Once the winter rains begin, I will hear the music of Mission Creek.

Yesterday, at the end of the month, the clouds thickened during the day. In the afternoon, a few large drops fell. The air felt dense and heavy, maybe rich in negative ions which some say lifts the spirits.

Around 3 am, we awoke to a long roll of thunder. For the next hour, lightning and thunder alternated, until the lightning seemed to rip open the heavy undersides of the clouds releasing a torrent which in a few minutes left behind a half an inch of rain.

At the end of the day, the clouds had retreated back to the mountains.

It appears that at last I have the intemperate Santa Barbara I had expected — a Santa Barbara of sundowner winds gusting down canyons, landslides, firestorms and debris flows, floods, thunder ricocheting off the mountain sides, and on the coast, high surfs which rearrange beaches.

Is this the fall and winter which will end the drought? Such secrets are closely held. In the meantime, I look often at the sky, sniff the air, and even conger up promising clouds. It can't hurt.

SOME OF THE BIRDS WHICH ARRIVE IN THE FALL

White-crowned Sparrow

Ruby-crowned Kinglet

Hermit Thrush

Townsend's Warbler

Looking Back — Winter After All

When one of my friends fell on an icy path this morning and Gibraltar Dam flowed over its spillway, the first time since 2011, I decided that winter could not be ignored.

I hadn't considered writing about Santa Barbara in the winter thinking that the season had been mostly passed by in these years of drought. Then yesterday, December 23, we had a storm that was worthy of qualifying as a winter storm in every way. The day began with a thin cloud cover which built during the morning to promising layers of clouds and brief gusts of wind, which by noon led to rain. After slacking off in a way that I had become used to during these dry years, the rain built again as if to defy my pessimism. By mid-afternoon the rain built to a real gully-washer. I was lucky enough to be in my car so I could enjoy splashing through flows of water at every intersection and best of all, seeing Mission Creek coursing down its creek bed after so many months of being bone dry.

From the sound of my bamboo wind chimes during the night, I knew the storm had passed to the east and the wind had

Storm-swollen Mission Creek at Tallant Road bridge

Lake Cachuma in a winter storm

shifted to the north as it does along the coast after a rain storm. The cold wind continues today pushing around remnant clouds, now empty of their contents.

I know storm must follow storm to make the creek a winter feature and the soil be soaked enough to start recharging the depleted water table. Lake Cachuma which lies in the valley between our mountains, the Santa Ynez, and the higher range to the east, is the reservoir which holds our water supply. At present, it's almost no lake at all, having shrunk to less than 7% of its capacity. Vultures have taken to roosting on the rim of the dam.

December ended with the rainfall slightly above normal.

January was another matter altogether thanks to massive storms brought across the Pacific by an atmospheric river — a new word in my weather lexicon. An atmospheric river can be several thousand miles long to a few hundred miles wide. Drawing up moisture from near the Hawaiian Islands, the warm air can transport large amounts of rain. It's what we once called the "Pineapple Express."

The atmospheric rivers produced five days of good rains. At the end of January, rainfall for the month was 8.96 inches rather than a normal 2.86 inches. Even the lawns, most of which were allowed to go brown over the summer and fall, were green again

The rains continued intermittently until Friday, February 17 The papers were advertising that the biggest storm of the season was on its way. Over the years, I have learned to be suspicious

An atmospheric river arrives on the California coast

of such a build-up which often leads to disappointment. I believe in sneaker storms — the ones which arrive with little

High surf is often part of a storm system

Mission Creek in flood at Botanic Garden. Photo courtesy of the Santa Barbara Botanic Garden

Flood water flowing over Indian Dam in the Botanic Garden. Photo courtesy of the Santa Barbara Botanic Garden

or no advance warning. That may be the old days before sophisticated weather-measuring equipment and computers, which can put together predictive models eliminating much of the guesswork.

At 5 AM heavy rain was falling, serious, confident rain. By mid-morning the velocity of the rain continued to increase. Coarse and dense raindrops were being driven by gale winds from the south-east. By early afternoon, the rain had slackened enough to allow me to drive down to the Mission Creek just below us. Others had already gathered. Some of us stood on the bridge itself which was trembling with the force of the volume of water pouring a few feet beneath. On the opposite side of the bridge where the stream bed is narrowed by rock walls, boulders were being slammed together. The percussive, booming sounds resembled thunder. Some people, unnerved by the violence, hurried back to their cars. As a fan of such drama, I stayed put.

The storm finally moved on leaving 5-inches of rain downtown and heavier amounts on the mountain slopes. Mission Creek up Mission Canyon left its stream bed and temporarily carved out a new route. Further engorged by a cargo of mud, the stream poured over the old Indian Dam.

The gift for me was that Mission Creek became a real stream, a winter stream which flowed for weeks on end, not just for a day or two after a rain.

Now it's early April and the creek has ceased to flow. It survived for few more days as isolated pools, until it disappeared altogether. I like to think that it continues to flow underground bringing moisture to the roots of the sycamores and to the other streamside plants.

A Perfect Spring

After such a sumptuous winter how could it not be — a perfect spring.

I came to Santa Barbara to live in September 2013, the second year of the drought. The landscape was dry, but as a native Californian, I expected dryness. The winter rains the next two years were scanty. Not only did the garden lawns die by intent, but landscape and street trees began suffering. Many of the redwoods, never a good choice for this semi-arid climate, were dying. The conifers were the hardest hit. The native ponderosa pines on Figueroa Mountain all succumbed, probably weakened by the drought and then attacked by the deadly bark beetle.

To try and save street trees, the city attached green plastic reservoirs to young trees which slowly released water to the roots.

Maybe several times during the winter, enough rain would fall to feed the headwaters of various creeks. Mission Creek with its springs high on mountain sides above the Botanic Garden came briefly to life with muddy torrents of water which rushed down the dry creek bed. Quickly depleted, the flow stopped and by the second day, the creek became isolated pools. By the third day, the creek disappeared all together.

Hills near Carrizo Plain

California poppies

Bush Lupine

With the return to silent stretches of dry rock, my spirits fell. I realized again how above all the landscape features — hills, mountains, valleys, and especially the noisy, restless ocean — it is creeks I love the best, for their cheerful sounds and their ability to be a magnet for surrounding life.

Spring in California is mostly about wildflowers, but in one of the ironies of a wet spring, grass and weeds growing tall often concealed the flowers. Figueroa Mountain had some nice displays, particularly where lupine grew on perennial shrubs or where poppies grew on serpentine soil which inhibits the rampant growth of grass.

It was in the semi-desert areas like Carizzo Plain, an hour and a half drive inland from San Luis Obispo, where the flowers were amazing, enough so, to gain the title — superbloom. Hills and the desert floors look as if they'd been splashed with paint.

But it is in the exuberance of the commoner plants that I saw the results of a wet winter. The wild oats, now going to seed are waist high, and must compete for space with wild radishes and Italian thistle.

After four years of drought that tested their endurance, allowing no luxury like new growth, live oaks this spring were transformed with explosions of tender bright green leaves. The shiny leaves concealed the coarse and somber, dark green foliage, some of which could now be shed.

New spring growth and flowers on the live oaks

Live oaks are the most abundant native tree of Samarkand, Oak Park and most lowland locations.

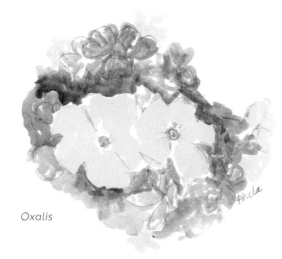

Oxalis

Nasturiums

Best of all was to see Mission Creek behaving like a real stream, not with just the episodic flow of two days that followed a rain during the preceding drought years. My morning ritual was to look through my binoculars into the small gap between the trees where I could see the overlapping brightness of moving water. The stream had a rhythm, sometimes squeezing around rocks making music and then released, spreading out in quiet pools, before being narrowed again. I think I could write a score with the proper notations.

The male oak flowers are heavy with pollen which will be released by the wind to fertilize some of the female flowers growing on the same tree. From the fertilized female flower comes the familiar acorn.

I imagine my father, who grew up near Oak Park, capturing tadpoles with a net, or creating a new flow by rearranging rocks. When the flow was strongest, he and his buddies, no doubt, fashioned miniature boats and then ran along the creek edge to see how they fared.

Two weeks after the last rain in March, the flow began to shrink, imperceptibly at first. But now in mid-April the creek has disappeared. Or, perhaps it flows beneath the surface still accessible to the roots of trees.

Oxalis, considered a hard-to-get-rid-of weed by most gardeners, crowded roadsides after this year's heavy rains.

Speculation has already begun about next winter. Through summer and early fall, conditions appear to be "neutral" with early signs of building El Nino conditions beginning later in the fall. In most years, a strong El Nino brings generous rains, but not always. Speculation, especially about future weather, is irresistible especially for weather buffs like myself.

In this most luxuriant of springs no slope is unclaimed. Near Samarkand, nasturtiums have naturalized a hillside.

JUNE 11, 2017

Less Than an Hour Away

Tucked into the coastal range 40 miles southeast of here, is a valley that fits my description of near perfection. The road which travels its length is five miles long. There are few buildings of any kind. Geographers would describe the countryside as oak/savanna. Only the fence lines tell you that the land has been claimed. On a good year of decent pasturage, you're apt to see some cattle and maybe men on horseback responsible for their well being.

Even its name Canada (pronounced canyada) Larga has a sweet resonance. "Canada" has a number of meanings: valley, glen, cattle trail. Take your pick. "Larga" is more specific, meaning long (or tall in another dimension).

The valley was part of a 6,658 acre Mexican land grant known as Canada Larga O Verde. Turning off highway 33 (one road to Ojai) onto Canada Larga Road you see your first bit of early California history — a 7-foor-high remnant of a rubble wall which was part of the aqueduct that once carried water seven miles from the Ventura River down to the the mission San Buenaventura where it satisfied the needs of the 350 inhabitants for their gardens and pastures. The waterworks were built by the Chumash Indians under the instruction from the padres sometime between 1785 and the early 1800s. What's left of the ruins is protected behind a chain link fence.

Not much remains of the nearby Canada Larga Creek in late spring but a sluggish

Remnant of the Old Aquaduct

PHILA ROGERS

Red-tailed Hawk's nest in eucalyptus

flow full of clots and streamers of algae. By the bridge, the creek runs beneath a steep slope of near white rock.

What interested us was the old, rather disreputable blue gum eucalyptus (actually several trees in various stages of decline). Ignoring the heaps of shed bark caught between branches, our focus was on a Red-tailed Hawk's nest with a full-grown young standing at its edge with an adult nearby. Nobody appeared happy with their presence. The Cassin's Kingbird with their nest in the same tree voiced their raucous objections, while a pair of Bullock's Orioles, with their nest in a smaller euc behind, went about their business of carrying food to their young.

I sat in the shade of a walnut orchard where ground doves were seen earlier and watched the activity. Getting back into the car, with windows down, we proceeded slowly up the narrow road stopping where there appeared to be activity. Birding along the Canada Larga Road is a challenge as the pullouts are infrequent and hardly adequate, and the occasional cars and trucks often travel at a high speed.

Bullock's Oriole, Western Kingbird

Lazuli Bunting

bird sitting on a rusty water tank. The bird turned out to be a Blue Grosbeak — one of the target birds of the trip. And best yet, it appeared to have food in its mouth. With young to raise, the pair should be around for a while.

Now I could indulge myself with the scenery and days later, at the computer, I would struggle for words adequate to describe what I was seeing. Maybe I should let it go and simply say that this landscape made me superbly happy.

Was it the contours and shapes of the hills, the close and distant views, the colors and always the possibility of an eagle? You're not going to be slammed by the brilliance of spring wildflowers. The muted tones of late spring reach a deeper place in one's feelings. Russets, pale beige grass, drifts of mustard reach up into gray chaparral with lavender undertones. A gifted landscape architect couldn't do it as well.

Barbwire fences make good perches and we were almost always in sight of a Western Kingbird, a low-slung bird with a yellow belly who would frequently leave its perch to grab something appetizing. One stop was warranted by a phainopepla calling from the upper branches of a half-dead walnut tree.

My eyes were on the yellow mustard growing along the fence where last year I had seen a dazzling Lazuli Bunting amongst the yellow flowers. Plenty of mustard this spring but no bunting. Further up the road everyone (but me) saw a smallish

Far to the northeast beyond the rounded hills, gave a glimpse of the higher mountains with their irregular profile. A fresh breeze filled my lungs and lifted hair away from my face. Two kingbirds flew close to a Raven's tail. My birding friend called it a "teaching lesson."

The road ended at a horse ranch. Now we were on level ground where we could rest in the shade of live oaks and sycamores with the bubbling songs of House Wrens surrounding us.

PHILA ROGERS

We planned on picnicking at a park along the Ventura River where we could count on Yellow Warblers singing in the sycamores and swallows with their small, bright voices sieving up insects over the water.

PHILA ROGERS

But I could only think about how nice it would be to set up my cot and roll out my bed roll under the edge of one of the oaks in the Canada Larga valley on a gentle slope with a view in all directions — perfect for night coming on with the changing colors. I could imagine crickets chirping in the dry grass and a small owl hooting nearby. Once darkness was complete I would observe stars undimmed by city lights and listen to a night wind rustling the oak leaves, bringing me far off scents.

PHILA ROGERS

Around the Corner to Nojoqui Falls

Sometimes it's only a few thin bands of water dropping 164 feet. Other times it's a gossamer tracery of water more mist than substance. It nourishes families of mosses and ferns growing on its walls. Only after a rain, does Nojoqui Falls aspire to something grander.

The falls (pronounced NAW- ho-wee) are named for a Chumash village "Naxuwi" once nearby.

When my granddaughter asked me what I wanted for my birthday, I said: "A day trip with you." We talked about where and decided on a drive up the coast and inland to Nojoqui Falls County Park, and then lunch at one of the good places in the Santa Ynez Valley. I wanted to walk along a creek and possibly even see falling water while it was still spring.

Driving up along the coast is a treat in itself. Once you've cleared the outskirts of Goleta you are in full view of the ocean and if the day is clear enough, you can see the profile of the islands on the horizon.

On the right, the Santa Ynez Mountains make a formidable barrier to the sea and its cool breezes. We passed three beach parks. On the landward side of the freeway, the beaches become canyons. Though beautiful on its own, the landscape stimulated memories — El Capitan Beach where grandson Stuart always wanted his birthday to be celebrated with a campout.

Nojoqui Falls

Surf at Refugio Beach

Just beyond Refugio Beach, the highway swings inland where ahead, the mountain wall is pierced by the Gaviota Tunnel. I thought about all those years when Santa Barbara could only be approached easily from the south.

PHILA ROGERS

At the sign "Nojoqui Falls County Park," we left the noisy highway and dropped down to the Old Coast Highway and Alisal Road to the peace and quiet of farmlands. Once horse pastures, organic produce now grows in the soil enriched by manure.

Skirting the western edge of the mountains, we rounded the corner to the lush, north-facing slopes, the rainiest place in the county. How different from the south-facing slopes above Santa Barbara where the mountain slopes are dominated by bare sandstone and chaparral.

When we turned into the park with its broad meadow and a scattering of trees, Granddaughter Caroline said: "This reminds me of Yosemite Valley." I could see her point except that when every detail of a beloved place like Yosemite is so perfectly embedded in my memory, nothing can compare.

We drove up to the end of the road where a few cars were parked. At the base of the

canyon, a short trail leads up to the falls.. Starting up the trail I was transported to the Berkeley Hills where bay trees also form arches of fragrant leaves and the sun shines through the thin leaves of the big-leaved maples. The creek burbling over dark rocks reminded me of the dark-gray basalts of home.

The final ascent on stone steps to the base of the falls looked damp, making them especially perilous for my old legs. A bench at their base invited me to sit a while, and let my granddaughter trot ahead while I listened to the creek and the cascade of Warbling Vireo songs spilling down from the bay trees overhead.

Stairs leading up to falls

Warbling Vireo

Purple Martin

Purple Martins, our largest and highest-flying swallow perform breath-taking acrobatics when hunting insects. At the park, Martins ignore man-made boxes in favor of holes in the sycamore trees.

Three weeks later with Berkeley birding friends, Bob Lewis and his wife, Hanno, we returned to Nojoqui Falls park to find the Purple Martins. While Bob sits on the lawn, I lie on my side watching Martins in flight. Stretched out, has become my preferred position for watching birds of the sky and for general cloud-spotting. (I highly recommend to others who love clouds "The Cloudspotter's Guide by Gavin Pretor-Pinney — the founder of The Cloud Appreciation Society)

Now, we will be leaving the park to the summer crowds, returning in the fall to see the winter birds like the beautiful Varied Thrush.

Varied Thrush

Birds watching birdwatcher watching birds

A Family Vacation at Big Bear Lake

After having lived most of my life in the Bay Area, California mountains meant only the Sierra Nevada. My earliest memories are of Lake Tahoe with the bands of blue, the color deepening the further the water was from shore. I remember the translucency of the water, the whiteness of the beach sand and the way the sun shining through the water left a dazzling pattern on the sandy bottom. And the granite, always angular and glistening with feldspar

Vacation in the mountains was a reprieve from home and the rank eucalyptus odors. Now it was sage and pine, and brilliant, hard-edged cumulus instead of the dull sheets of stratus.

But it was time to put all that behind and turn my thoughts without aversion to the Southern California Mountains, and another transverse mountain range, the San Bernadinos. The deep power of the San Andreas fault had twisted the mountains sideways, contrary to the northwest trending of most other California ranges.

With some of the family now living in Southern California, a three and a half hour drive to Big Bear Lake in the San Bernardinos won the day over nine hours north to Lake Tahoe.

The San Bernardino Mountains rise abruptly on all sides out of its arid landscape. The curving road makes a quick ascent passing occasional coulter and knobcone pines, dried stalks of yuccas and chaparral. In a land of few lakes, only dams can create a body of water, gathered mostly from snow melt. Big Bear Lake, no exception, occupies its own shallow valley set in low mountains and open conifer forests. Unlike the Sierra, where millions of trees have succumbed to the long drought and insect attacks, Big Bear's trees look healthy, perhaps being accustomed to dry years.

ROGER BRADFIELD

Grams and Grandson

While noticing the distinct differences between the appearance of Sierra Nevada and the San Bernardinos, I remembered

San Bernardino Mountains

reading of their similarities. Both began as batholiths formed of cooling magma deep underground before being uplifted some three million years ago. Older rocks overlain the newer granites. But in the Sierra Nevada, the old rock eroded away with the heavier rains and the extensive glaciation. In the Santa Bernardinos, with glaciation only on the highest peaks and less rain, more of the old rock remains.

Because we were nine people, we rented a large, recently remodeled house which is currently on the market for three and a half million dollars. While the family took to kayaks and paddle boards. I settled in on the deck to figure out this place.

The dominate pine is the Jeffrey — a close relative of the ponderosa (yellow) pine, which along with the coulter pine, are all members of the yellow pine family distinguished by packets of three long needles which produce nice harmonies in the wind.

The fir family was represented by white fir growing, at the deck rail, with short, dense needles which point upward. Each species seems to have its own distinct odor. Press your nose into the cracks between the plates of bark on the yellow pine and you smell vanilla. Sniff the white fir and you get an essence of pine and citrus. Be like the native American Indians, brew a cup of tea with the needles and you have your daily requirement for vitamin C.

But what took my fancy was the pair of sugar pines above a neighbor's roof. Aside from being both the largest and second tallest in the pine family with uncommonly long pine cones, I love this pine. John Muir savored the exuded gum which he said  was sweeter than maple-syrup. The branches are arranged on the straight trunk often symmetrically, but sometimes a branch will shun order and stretch out further than the rest. Cones hang near the tip of the branch. I remember watching them in a winter wind swaying as if they were extravagant ornaments. Once, while examining a cone a foot and a half long lying on the ground, I remember someone telling me that the scales expand and contract with the change of temperature and the prickles make a grove in the soil for the seed. I've never been able to find another citation for that charming "fact" since.

The forest, at least in the neighborhood of our house on north-facing shore is knitted together by an understory of a tall manzanita called Pringle Manzanita. The season for its pink, urn-shaped flowers is long past and only a few dried berries remain.

Time to shake off the lethargy that comes with an occasional fleecy cloud drifting across the blue and then dissolving or the soft song of pines, and explore the rest of the lake. The dam is a modest one required

Manzanita

PHILA ROGERS

PHILA ROGERS

PHILA ROGERS

It appears there would be no avoiding the walk once my daughter learned of it. Children, no matter how old themselves, are reluctant to entertain the ills (real or imagined) of their elders. I did bring my boots so maybe I can avoid a compound fracture when I turn my ankle on the inevitable loose rock.

Once we turned off the road that circles the lake, we were in the forest headed uphill. We pitched and heaved over the bumpy road. But once in this sub-alpine forest we felt like we were back in the forests above Lake Tahoe. Though I am considered the Chief Exclaimer in the family, we all exclaimed over this familiar beauty. No more yellowish rock. Here the granitic core of the mountain revealed itself. The understory became varied — sometimes tender green fields of bracken ferns, other times corn lilies.

We parked at the end of the road where a sign pointed downhill to the lodgepole pine and to the Bluff Lake Preserve. I recognized this kind of trail — decomposed granite made "interesting" by rocks and exposed roots. My grandson Stuart walked close behind me and my daughter ahead of me. I focused on what was underfoot allowing only sidelong glances at the creek next to the trail overhung with wildflowers, the first such sight in these mountains. The trail leveled out as we approached the lodgepole pine grove. Lodgepole pines are uncommon in this southern forest. They hark back to a cooler era. My joy was somewhat tempered by remembering that I had to walk back out. I didn't care. I hadn't expected this gift in my 89th year.

only to hold back the snow melt and the marshy waters in the shallow basin. Once around the corner to the drier south-facing shore, sages and the sturdy Sierra juniper make an appearance.

At the visitor's center, we take literature on the trees of the region and the description of a Champion Lodgepole Pine further up the mountain which sounds almost reachable by a short trail.

NANCY LAW

NANCY LAW

"We made it"

Two oldtimers

The old giant was closely encircled by younger trees (as I am by my family). The tree overlooks a broad green meadow—a meadow which not so long ago had been a pond. In the Sierra, the Lodgepole pine is the first to show up as the pond becomes a meadow. As other trees move in, the meadow becomes part of the forest.

The noble tree is a part of a national registry of the largest known of its species in a particular geographic area. A nearby Jeffrey pine is several hundred years old, an "old growth" survivor in a forest that had been heavily logged.

PHILA ROGERS

The Best For Last

For the last four years, I have written about Santa Barbara's seasons, landscapes, and sometimes history. But what has really commanded my imagination during all this time have been the Channel Islands.

On infrequent childhood visits to Santa Barbara during the summer to visit my grandmother's apartment, two blocks from the beach, or my cousin's house in the hills, I usually came alone from Oakland on the Southern Pacific Daylight train.

I have no recollection of seeing the islands. Even though mountainous Santa Cruz Island was only 25 miles offshore, it, and its neighboring islands, were usually hidden by a bank of fog.

What I remember most was the beach, the bright city lights from my cousin's house, the pale flakes of ash that my aunt said were coming from a fire in the mountains.

It was not until I was an adult, when two of my three children had settled in Santa Barbara, that the islands became familiar to me. Most often, the plane approaching the airport made a wide arc over the ocean and the islands in order to land into the prevailing wind.

Santa Cruz Island in the spring, mainland in background

BILL DEWEY

Satellite View of the Channel Islands

From then on, I was eager to find some way of getting out to the islands. Santa Cruz Island, the largest, was mostly privately owned by the Stanton family of Los Angeles. The second largest island, Santa Rosa Island, was owned and operated as a cattle ranch by Vail and Vickers, whose boats sometimes brought cattle to the mainland at Santa Barbara. San Miguel, the northernmost island off Point Conception, a windy place surrounded by a turbulent sea, was famous mostly for its huge population of seals and sea lions, drawn to the cold, upwelled water rich in nutrients.

I remembered from the family stories that both my mother and father as children had visited Santa Cruz Island. Before she died in 1981, I asked my mother to tell me her story.

On lined yellow paper, she wrote in her spidery hand: *"When I was a small girl the trip to the Santa Barbara islands was a great adventure. One time my mother, grandmother and little brother went to Santa Cruz Island in a fishing boat. As The Channel was very rough that day, the deep dips into the troughs of the waves were terrifying to all of us. The kindly Italian fisherman tried to reassure us but we did not regain our equilibrium until we landed safely on the island.*

Eaton's Resort at Pelican Bay — 1920

At night we could hear the wild pigs rooting around in the underbrush which was scary.

The food in the dining tent was plain but good with plenty of fresh fish. A highlight of our stay was the trip into the blue caves. One entered their inner fastnesses in rowboats. These caves were accessible only at low tide and in quiet waters. Within them, the water was a brilliant blue which became darker the further in we ventured. It was thrilling to trail one's hand which yielded a ghostly phosphorescence. Back home again I had much to tell my less venturesome playmates."
— Elaine Adrian Willoughby

I knew less about my father's trip (or trips) to Santa Cruz Island. There was something about a borrowed Boston whaler, and that the wild boar they shot was so tightly wedged in a narrow canyon that they had to butcher it on site and deliver it piecemeal to the boat.

I can imagine that Santa Barbara in the early 1900s, with less than 10,000 inhabitants, was an ideal place for a boy to grow up. He and several co-conspirators built a shack up San Roque canyon until a wildfire destroyed it. I have a small photo of him as a young teenager with his dad on a mountain trail, he with high boots, a slouch hat, and a canvas rucksack hanging heavily off his shoulders.

Now it was my turn.

Sea Cave

TWO WHO CELEBRATE THE NATURAL WORLD

Hugh Ranson — birder, teacher, and writer who writes the Saturday column "Bird Watch" for the Santa Barbara News Press. He began his birdwatching as a boy in England.

In the last five years, he has taken up the study of dragonflies and during lunch breaks can often be found at a local pond with his net and camera.

Bill Dewey — Bill has been photographing the California landscape since the early 1970s and has been flying since the 1980s. Some of his favorite subjects include the California Channel Islands, Carrizo plain, Baja California, and the rural California landscape. His work is widely published and shown in various galleries and museums. His aerial photos begin each of my Santa Cruz Island sections

ROE ANNE WHITE

BILL DEWEY

See some of Bill Dewey's glorious photos on his website — www.billdeweyphoto.com

SANTA CRUZ ISLAND — THEN AND NOW

The Archipelago of the four Northern Channel Islands includes westernmost San Miguel Island, Santa Rosa Island, the mountainous Santa Cruz Island, and finally little Anacapa with its "tail" of broken islets trailing behind. Now that I've settled in Santa Barbara where I most likely will conclude my life, I view the islands from the mainland, always drawn outward toward them. I see them from my daughter's house high on the hillside above Mission Canyon, most often reclining on the horizon in their bed of haze. Sometimes the fog obscures them from view altogether, or there are times when the vapors are swept away by a dry north wind, and I can clearly see their cliffs and coves.

Over the years I've collected my own experiences of the islands. Last year, in May, I crossed the choppy Channel on an Island Packers boat out of Ventura Harbor. I was lucky enough to have secured an invitation to the annual mass, thanks to Marla Daily, the head of the Santa Cruz Island Foundation.

The Northern Channel Islands from the air, with Anacapa in the foreground, Santa Cruz, Santa Rosa, and San Miguel Island in the background. Photo by Bill Dewey

Mass at the chapel

But my awareness of the islands, particularly Santa Cruz Island, began as a child when I read The Channel Islands of California, by Charles F. Holder, published in 1910, which I claimed from my parents' library. The book with its turquoise-blue linen cover and the decorative drawings of flying fish is now on my Santa Barbara bookshelf. I still love to reread the description of the ride in a horse-drawn carriage up the wild canyon to the Central Valley from the anchorage at Prisoners' Harbor.

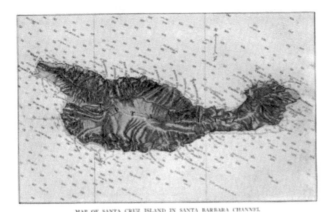

MAP OF SANTA CRUZ ISLAND IN SANTA BARBARA CHANNEL

From "The Channel Islands of California"

Quoting from the book: *From the sea, Santa Cruz Island is a jumble of lofty hills and mountains, with deep gorges and canyons winding in every direction.*

Hidden away in the very heart of the island is an ideal ranch, with a pronounced foreign atmosphere, in a climate as perfect as that of Avalon to the south.

Seated in the trap, with our host holding the reins, we turned into a gorge... the road wound upward; the horses now splashing through the summer stream beneath gnarled and picturesque oaks, now out into the open, where the sun poured down through rifts in the canyon beneath a sky of tender blue, plunging into the narrow canyon again, where walls grew lofty and precipitous, shutting out the glare of sunlight. The stream bed was dry the first mile or so but then we encountered water. We forded the stream several times before the canyon sides and the mountains suddenly melted away. Three miles of

this, and the charming canyon road came to an abrupt end. The horse dashed into a long, rolling valley, where the air was like velvet on the cheek and an incense of flowers and vines filled the nostrils.

But last Sunday it was in the cab of battered green truck driven by one of Marla's relatives. Several trucks of various vintages were waiting for passengers who had disembarked from the boat tied up at the end of the long pier. I carefully climbed up the ladder, aided by the crew, to the rough planks of the pier. I was more uncertain than usual because I had fallen on the deck of the boat when

PHILA ROGERS

PHILA ROGERS

Approaching the pier at Prisoners' Harbor

a sudden lurch had tossed me down on my back.

I'd been pulled back upright without apparent injury though my confidence in staying upright had been challenged.

It was different from when Holder had made the same trip at least a hundred years earlier. No longer a working ranch, most of the island now belongs to the Nature Conservancy. The vineyards which once traced the contours of the hills had been removed. Gone were the horses, cattle, and sheep. The ranch house was no longer ornamented with the iron grilles from the ranch forge.

The people this day were mainlanders who had come to enjoy the annual festivities, attend mass, drink wine and feast on the barbecue before returning to the mainland on the four o'clock boat.

I mostly kept to myself, listening for bird songs and calls and finally spotting an Island fox. Mostly, I tried to recapture in these dry hills the island of my dreams.

The ranch house in the Central Valley. Photo courtesy of the Santa Barbara Botanic Garden

SALLY ISAACSON

A TRIP ON ISLAND PACKERS FROM VENTURA TO SANTA CRUZ ISLAND

Leaving the mainland behind

Approaching Santa Cruz Island, Anacapa to the Left

Hills surrounding the Central Valley

PHILA ROGERS

Giant Kelp

BILL DEWEY

THIS TIME FOR WORK

I'm drawn to all islands, but especially to those that lie off a mainland shore, like the Channel Islands. At times they beguile you, half hidden behind veils of fog, and at other times they abandon subtlety, revealing in dazzling detail their pale sea cliffs and shadowed canyons.

I don't pretend to understand the power these islands have on me. Maybe it was the epic tales of sea voyages and island landfalls that fueled my imagination as a young reader. Or the stories told by my parents, who were raised in Santa Barbara. I made my first crossing to Santa Cruz Island, the largest island of the northern group, 25 years ago on a three-masted schooner. Since then I have managed to return often, usually as a participant in natural history groups or as a Nature Conservancy volunteer. Last spring, I volunteered as a plant monitor, and saw the island once again, this time from the back of a jeep as we lurched over ridgetop dirt roads on our way to inventory plants.

Near Christy Ranch

BILL DEWEY

High road on the red rock ridge with Santa Rosa Island in the distance. Photo courtesy of the Santa Barbara Botanic Garden

STEVE WINDHAGER

To the north was a mountain range of ruddy-colored volcanic rock. To the south toward the open sea rose a conical mountain peak of dazzling white rock known as the Blanca Volcanics. The island is, in fact, made up of two disparate land masses, that came from different directions and are sutured together by a fault known as the Central Valley Fault. It is not hard to believe that this wild jumbled Technicolor landscape is still on the move, sliding northward toward the Aleutians. Some 18,000 years ago when the ocean level was lower, all four islands of the northern group were joined together in one super-island scientists refer to as "Santarosae". Through the islands' evolution many configurations developed, but they have not been joined to the mainland, at least not in recent geological times.

The plants and animals we see on Santa Cruz Island today came on the winds, were carried by ocean currents, or were brought ashore by human visitors. Salamanders and other stowaways came ashore on the same log rafts that the Chumash fashioned into canoes. Once on the island, many animals and plants have evolved distinctive forms.

On our trips around the island, we saw the little island fox that weighs barely three pounds. Other species are larger than their mainland cousins — examples of what scientists call gigantism. The Santa Cruz Island jay, for example, is bluer and 25 percent larger than the mainland Scrub Jay. Toyons and elderberries are shrubs or small trees on the mainland, but they can grow to 40-60 feet on the island. Maybe it's the moderate temperature, moist climate or lack of competitive species. I call it island exuberance. There are fewer species too, fewer kinds of birds, two types of snakes, and no burrowing animals at all. The four terrestrial animals are endemic, meaning they are found no place else.

(First published as *Island Exuberance* for *Santa Barbara Magazine*, Spring 1994)

JONI KELLEY

Island Fox. Photo courtesy of the Santa Barbara Botanic Garden

SANTA CRUZ ISLAND: THE CALIFORNIA GALAPAGOS

By Hugh Ranson

I recently ventured out to Santa Cruz Island in search of migrant birds. While I didn't see a great variety of migrants, there were enough resident species to keep me well entertained. Island foxes, which have made quite a comeback, trotted about throughout the day, seemingly unconcerned by human intrusion. Another island endemic, the Island Scrub Jay, was much in evidence.

Hundreds of birders venture out to the island each year to see the jay. Why? It's a species found nowhere else on earth. The Island Scrub Jay was once considered conspecific with the California Scrub Jay, the familiar jay found commonly along our coast. It was officially recognized as a separate species in 1998. It is larger, much more brilliantly blue, has a larger beak, a different voice, and different social habits than its coastal cousin.

There are at least a couple of theories as

One of the acorn-eating island scrub-jays.

to how the jay made its way to the island and began the slow differentiation from the mainland species. Jays are weak fliers and do not travel across large bodies of water. One thought is that jays made their way by hitching rides on floating vegetation. Another is that during a period of glaciation, when sea levels were lower, jays were able to cross the much narrower channel. At any rate, it is thought island jays have been isolated from the mainland for over 150,000 years.

Santa Cruz Island has a healthy population of jays estimated at 2,300 individuals. However, this population is considered vulnerable because of the small area of the island. There is the constant danger of fire, and more menacing still, the threat of West Nile Virus, to which corvids (jays are in the crow family) are particularly susceptible. Because of this latter threat, many of the jays have been captured and vaccinated.

It seems the Island Scrub Jay is perhaps even more remarkable than we realized. Recently, biologist Kate Langin made a discovery that turned a theory of evolution on its head. She found that there are two separate populations of jays on the island, one that favors oak woodland, and one that inhabits pine forests. The oak-loving jays feed largely on acorns and have evolved shorter, stouter bills. The pine-inhabiting jays have longer, narrower bills, adapted for extracting pine nuts from pinecones. Even where pine and oak woodland are mere yards apart, the two populations appear to remain separate.

Charles Darwin theorized that in order for species to differentiate, like the famous Galapagos finches, there needs to be

Ironwood Grove. Photo courtesy of the Santa Barbara Botanic Garden

STEVE WINDHAGER

geographic separation. The island jays appear to be the first known instance where this theory doesn't hold.

If you haven't yet made it out to Santa Cruz Island, it's time you did! Island Packers of Ventura run daily trips to the island. It takes a little over an hour to reach the island, and there are excellent opportunities for viewing marine mammals and birds on the crossing. There are two anchorages served by the company, Scorpion and Prisoners. You have an excellent chance of seeing the jay at Prisoners. It used to be that they were rarely seen at Scorpion, but in recent years they have become more common there, frequently foraging in the campground. I saw several there on my last visit. Scorpion also has many choices for coastal walking trails.

This article and photo was excepted from "Bird Watch," published each Saturday in the Santa Barbara News Press.

The ironwood tree is a native to the Channel Islands, the scalloped-edged ironwood leaf resembles the splayed foot of the American Coot. The light ripples as the tall trees sway in the sea breeze. In the presence of these shaggy-barked survivors, you can imagine these to be sacred groves. Islands have a way of compressing — and enlarging — human emotions, and island tales are replete with mysterious and sometimes tragic human stories. In the singularity of an island, you confront your own separateness, you own uniqueness. It's been almost a year since my last island visit. Every day here on the mainland, I climb the hill behind my house to look seaward, hoping for a glimpse of the dark shapes on the horizon — elated when I can see them, a little lonely when they are obscured by fog or clouds.

TWO JAYS

The Island Scrub Jay was once thought to be a sub-species of our common coastal California Scrub Jay, but now is recognized as a separate species. The Channel Islands have been separated for eons from the mainland. Jays being weak flyers, and with 25 miles of channel separating them, the Island Scrub Jay has had a long time to develop its separate characteristics.

The Island jay is over all bigger (the beak especially so), the plumage is brighter and bluer and its cheek is near-black instead of gray.

Island Scrub Jay

HUGH RANSON

California Scrub Jay

BOB LEWIS

NOVEMBER 2018

Where I Live

Early November
The resident hawk
Repeats its urgent calls.
Where is the rain?
The temperature is above eighty
Night falls with red skies
Color caught by the high cirrus clouds
Too thin for rain.

With darkness comes
The cricket stridulations
The final notes in the fading season

After midnight I step out on my porch,
Looking high to the south
Orion waits, trailed by Sirius,
The hunter's faithful dog.

Venus will soon separate itself from the
    rising sun
And before month's end will shine alone
In the eastern sky.

Once I'd imagined spending my final years
In the town where I was born
In a tiny house of my own design
One room only
With alcoves for bathing, sleeping,
    fixing tea
A steep roof with a skylight or two
A generous porch under a sheltering eave.
High in the Berkeley Hills,

Instead, my final years
Will be spent in Santa Barbara

To the west, the sunset

PHILA ROGERS

After the storm

PHILA ROGERS

in a spacious apartment
One of many apartments
For elders like myself,
Close to family
a hedge against loneliness.

The geographer in me
Wants to tell you
That Santa Barbara is located
At the southern end of Central California.
Maybe 50 miles below Pt Conception
Where the coast bends inland
Thanks to the San Andreas Fault
Flexing its muscles.
So now the coastal mountains run
From east to west,
and most confusing of all
You look south if you want to see
    the ocean.

For me, the ocean has always been
    to the west,
In the direction of the setting sun
Where if you sail far enough
You'll bump into China.

The high Santa Ynez Mountains to
    the North
shields the town from certain
    cold draughts,
but in downpours the mountains
shed all manner of debris
from silt to sandstone boulders
as big as cars.

Now as an amateur geologist,
I'll tell you that this knoll
I call home, is surrounded
By flatter lands referred to
As an alluvial fan,
Crossed by creeks that
Only show up when it rains.

Locals brag about the mild climate
Forgetting about those vehement
    moments
Of gale-force winds
Called sundowners.
or what about the microbursts
Which have been known to knock a plane
Out of the sky?

94

And there's nothing mild about my
    landscape.
Never still — it twists, heaves and cracks.
Worse, it is said that all the commotion
Is bringing Los Angeles ever closer.

Once we were covered by a warm sea
With dinosaurs wandering the shallows
later mountains rose up,
Full of sea shells.

Now it seems that our future is drought.

I look out the east-facing windows
Down into Oak Park with its
Pale limbed-sycamores and faded foliage.

It's a peoples' park
With mariachis on the weekend
Shouting children
Birthdays with piñatas
Quinceaneras, sometimes a funeral

Look up to the first ridge
To St. Anthony's towers
To the two rosy domes
Of the old mission.

Look further to the mountain bulk
The Santa Ynez and the conical shape
Of my mountain – Montecito Peak

East view

And how the angled sun
Deepens its canyons.

Slide your eyes sideways
To where the mountains
Slip into the blue line of the sea.

Now face south
Over our native garden
Bordered by the oaks from the park
To the silent creek bed.
I look for hummingbirds, bush rabbits
and worry about coyotes

The east hills, called the Mesa
Hold off the fog
Until after dark,
when the hills are breached.

Oh yes, my garden off the front door
The narrow porch of a garden,
Hung with red geraniums
And softened by pots of ferns.
I lie in my bed beneath the windows

Foggy day

Hoping for wind to move the chimes.
I lift my head at dawn
Do I see the silhouette of the mountains
Against the lightening sky?

Or are we cocooned in the fog
That drips from trees
Almost as welcome as rain.

And what is the first bird this morning?
The clink of the towhee
The querulous wren
The sweet ring of sparrows' song?

Now you are hearing the voice of the birder
Leaning on every song
In the absence of clear sight

Acorn woodpecker, flicker
With strong beak and loud call
Or the relentless caw of the black crow
Boss of the neighborhood?

Will I be lucky enough
To have an owl's hoot rouse me
In the early morning hour?

I feather my nest
With a down comforter
books
Bouquets of pungent sage
Baskets of lichen.

How do I finish this short tale?
A day ending, I suppose.
With the dark coming on by five
A tale of rain arriving?

A gusty wind from the southeast
Testing itself.

In the early morning hours
Between midnight and dawn
The rain falls
I smell it first
The sweet fragrance of hope

Could this be
The beginning of a season
Of abundant rains
Enough to end the drought?

Clockwise from top: rainbow, looking into native plant garden, finches feeding on niger seeds, mission creek, sunrise from the apartment

Nature's Note

SHORT, SEASONAL SELECTIONS

PHILA ROGERS

Uncertain September

For the first couple of weeks of the new month, September seemed more like an extension of summer. But don't be fooled, change is at hand. September is more likely to be erratic with often the hottest days of the year and more days with dry offshore winds, carrying desert scents. With the twin demands of raising broods and molting over, birds, in an adventurous spirit, are leaving familiar haunts. Don't be surprised to see the brilliant Western Tanager visiting your bird bath.

For sure evidence of seasonal change, look to the sky. As the sun lowers into the southern sky, it shines each day further into our south-facing windows. Venus, last month low in the western sky, is now the morning star. Getting up at dawn and looking above the mountains to the east, you will be rewarded with lovely Venus at its brightest.

I have a special affection for the gregarious winter sparrows. First to arrive are usually the White-crowned Sparrows who fill our gardens with their sweet songs as they call back and forth to one another. White-crowned Sparrows are unique in that they have a different dialect according to where they were born.

By next month, fall will most surely have arrived.

*Reprinted from **Sam News**, September 2015*

PHILA ROGERS

Fire!

So far, we've managed to escape a major fire this season. But with the rains unlikely to arrive before November, the danger is not over. Vegetation is tinder-dry and the season of heat and dry winds is still with us. With our steep, chaparral covered mountains, we live in one of the most fire-prone areas in the world. Add to the mix, the sundowner winds, which originate in the Santa Ynez Valley, can sometimes roar down the canyons late in the day.

Our last major fire, the Jesusita Fire in May 2009, began in the hills above Mission Canyon. Before it was over, thousands of people had to be evacuated, 78 houses were lost, 22 other heavily damaged, and 6,733 acres had been burned.

My family and their neighbors were evacuated to a beach-side motel, where for several days they maintained a vigil before the television, desperate for news about their home (theirs was saved but not all their neighbors were so lucky).

Aided by cooling temperatures and rising humidity from the onshore winds, the fire was finally stopped at Foothill Road. But who could forget the eerie orange light, the pungent odor, and the showers of pale ash during those terrible days. And the towering pyrocumulus cloud formed when the smoke rose high into the atmosphere.

As a survivor of the 1989 Berkeley-Oakland Hills fire, I can't help but glance often up to the mountains looking for that first plume of smoke, hoping that the rains begin early.

*Reprinted from **Sam News**, October 2015*

PHILA ROGERS

Young big-leafed maple in Mission Creek

The Turning of the Season

"Fall migration has begun," (From "Bird Watch" by Karen Bridger, August 13, News-Press)

What a welcome phrase! To know that the summer doldrums are ending, with the tedious pattern of sun and fog. With the fall equinox later in the month, the new season officially begins. Seasonal changes are subtle in coastal California where September and October days can be warmer than summer itself.

But what is changing is the light. The days have grown markedly shorter. And with the sun lower in the southern sky, shadows take on substance, and the landscape is looking more dense, more baroque, no longer flattened by a sun high overhead. If we lived up on the mountain, further from city lights, we would see that the star landscape has changed, too.

*Reprinted from **Sam News**, September 2016*

Mission Creek, dry and wet

What Will It Be?

Although our rainy season doesn't officially begin until November, we're all speculating about the winter ahead. Will it be another disastrously dry year or one with bountiful rainfall? The Farmers Almanac says look at the colored bands on the wooly caterpillar. The recent NOAA bulletin ENSO (for El Nino Southern Oscillation), though not a forecast, shows the measurements of the atmospheric pressure between the tropical eastern and western Pacific and the water temperatures. This winter season appears to be close to neutral, between the El Nino of last year, which disappointed us with low rainfall, and the La Nina with colder ocean temperatures and often a dry winter.

After six years, I'm saddened by the deepening drought with its dry creeks and dispirited trees with limp leaves. I like to imagine some night soon awakening to a rising southeast wind and then, YES, the sound of water dripping off the eaves, and wafting through the open window the ineffable aroma of the thirsty earth getting its first good soaking in months.

*Reprinted from **Sam News**, October 2016*

BOB LEWIS

*Red-shouldered
Hawk*

The Hawk That Never Shuts Up

It's hard to ignore that loud, persistent "keeyuur, keeyuur, keeyuur" that comes from Oak Park most days. Lately, I'm been hearing a more tentative call which I've decided is probably a juvenile — it's survival a feat when successfully raising a nestling surrounded by marauding crows.

Red-shouldered Hawks are not to be confused with the Red-tailed Hawk which often can be seen as it soars high overhead searching for movement below with its acute vision. Red-shouldered Hawks have shorter wings and longer tails than other members of the large buteo family of which the Red-tail is also member.

The Red-shouldered Hawk favors dense woods with clearings like Oak Park. The male when viewed front on when perching in one of our pines has a bright cinnamon-colored breast — a real standout in the generally brownish hawk family.

*Reprinted from **Sam News**, August 2017*

*Left to right: Toyon,
Band-tailed Pigeon*

The Harvest

At first I was puzzled by all the rustling in the tops of the live oaks below me until I saw the big Band-tailed Pigeons flying in and out of the trees. There was no sound except for the branchlets thrashing about and sometimes the clapping of wings. Then it came to me, of course, acorns. These big native pigeons love acorns, and ripe ones had been falling for a while, rolling about, dangerous underfoot.

And then there is the reddening of the"Christmas berries," (Heteromeles arbutifolias) or toyon as we call the shrub after the old Spanish word for canyon. Toyon is an important member of the local chaparral community, preferring the moister places like canyons. The prolific red berries are popular for holiday bouquets. In the Hollywood Hills the berries were so enthusiastically harvested that an ordinance was passed prohibiting picking. Our winter resident, the Hermit Thrush loves the berries and if its cousin the Robin (often accompanied by Cedar Waxwings) arrive in flocks, they can strip even a big bush in a day

*Reprinted from **Sam News**, October 2017*

NATURE WAKES UP

While September may have been
One of the somnolent months,
October is the month of awakening.
While the summer birds have slipped away
Quietly to their winter homes in the south,
The mountain and northern birds are
Arriving to take up their winter residence.

This is a carefree bunch
Done with nesting and molting
Ready to jostle a bit with fellow travelers
And with the locals for favorable winter territories
With the best berry bushes and seeds.

The mostly silent weeks are over.
Though without the bright plumage of spring,
The Yellow-rumped Warblers fill our gardens
With their busyness, and the tiny Ruby-crowned Kinglets
Flash their bright crowns for reasons of their own.

But it is the White-crowned Sparrows arriving
From the willow thickets in the far north,
Descending on our gardens, still full of spring song,
Delighting us and waking up the natural world,
Dulled by too much summer.

It's time to look to the sky
No more flat, gray stratus clouds we call fog.
Now it's aggregations of clouds of various shapes and elevations —
The high-altitude swirls of the ice clouds we call cirrus,
The collections of almost-identical mid-level clouds
Resembling sheep feeding in fields of blue.

By the end of the month,
Bright Venus will become our morning star
Giving us reason to arise at dawn to salute it
And its fellow travelers, just ahead of the reddening sky.

But over all, is the agonizing question —
Will there be enough rain to fill our creeks
And to bring us the green we crave?

*Reprinted from **Sam News**, October 2018*

PHILA ROGERS

Evergreen Pear
(Pyrus Kawakamii)

Santa Barbara is awash with white blooms — the early spring explosions of the evergreen pear. The tree lines the city streets, grows in gardens and parks, a tree which is easy to overlooked when shiny green leaves replace the flowers. In a mild coastal town like Santa Barbara, the tree is rarely completely deciduous.

The evergreen pear has its detractors. The leaves are often disfigured by black fungus spots and are often shed. Saying the shape of the tree is asymmetrical is one way of describing the unruly growth which often leads to branches cracking and falling. The small, bronze fruit is inedible.

But all is forgiven when in the short days of winter, the tree bursts into glorious bloom, and in the slightest breeze, petals fall like snow. Looking up though the near- black framework of branches and dazzling white flowers, makes the blue sky even bluer.

But don't push your nose into the petals, the odor is somewhat unpleasant and the feeding honeybees may resent your intrusion.

*Reprinted from **Sam News**, February 2015*

(LEFT TO RIGHT): BOB LEWIS, BOB LEWIS, TOM GINN

Left to Right: Anna's Hummingbird, Allen's Hummingbird, Rufous Hummingbird

Hummingbirds

I can't image a garden without hummingbirds. I'm lucky to live where flowers bloom year around so I'm always visited by these lovely birds. Hummingbirds are exclusively a bird of the Americas, with their highest concentration of species in the Andes.

Their aerial abilities, fueled by flower nectar, include being able to hover in place or change directions in an instant. With the highest metabolism of any animal, at night or when flowers are scarce, the hummer goes into a torpor to save energy.

Once mating takes place, the male leaves in search of new partners, and the female alone builds the nest and raises the young. Her nest includes spider's silk which is strong and flexible, so the nest can expand as the nestlings grow. In a final artistic touch, she uses lichens to decorate the exterior of the nest.

The Allen's Hummingbirds in Southern California, once only a summer resident, often no longer migrate south in the winter because local flowering plants are available in every season. The Rufous Hummingbirds who pass through Santa Barbara as spring migrants, travel as far north as Alaska. These bronze jewels have the longest migration of any hummingbird.

Though hummingbirds "song" is restricted to various buzzes and squeaks, they dazzle with their iridescent colors, lifting the spirits of even the casual observer.

*Reprinted from **Sam News**, June 2015*

TOM GINN

*White-crowned
Sparrow*

The Winter Birds

Undaunted by the fall heat, the winter birds have arrived. September brought the Yellow-rumped Warblers, their modest attire brightened by touches of yellow. They spend the winter months here gleaning through the trees, letting you know their location by frequents "jibs."

And now that minute dynamo has arrived — the Ruby-crowned Kinglet, barely four inches long, greenish in color, with white wing bars, a bright white eye ring, and the habit of flicking its wings. It conceals its ruby crown unless agitated, which seems often enough.

As others arrived from far-off places, I think about these small creatures, weighing only ounces, with hollow bones, traveling so many miles in response to an evolutionary imperative. I wish I lived away from city sounds so at night I could hear their small voices as they call back and forth, keeping track of one another in flight.

Consider our wintering White-crowned Sparrow, coming from its breeding grounds in the Alaska tundra, making the return trip in the spring, in the most dangerous venture of its avian life.

*Reprinted from **Sam News**, November 2015*

(LEFT TO RIGHT): BOB LEWIS, TOM GINN

Left to right: Hermit thrush feeding on toyon berries, Ruby-crowned Kinglet

The Dark Month

The days have been growing shorter since the end of June by about two minutes each day, giving us time to adjust. Then suddenly on November 6, daylight savings ends and our day abruptly ends at 5:30 pm. For the early risers, the change may appear to be a bonus. But not for long, as the days continue to grow shorter until the winter solstice.

And what to do in the long evenings? Like the birds, I'm ready to tuck my head under my wing and call it a day. That might have worked in the summer when the nights were eight hours long. Now, I look to the dark sky and admire the bright constellation Orion and his companions as they travel from north to south. And I wake up shortly after dawn, to hear the sweet song of the White-crowned Sparrow who has traveled from the far north where there is no daylight at all, to coastal California where life is easier. In a hurry? Sparrows have been recorded as traveling 300 miles in a night.

The sparrows are joined by other winter residents — the Hermit Thrush, Ruby-crowned Kinglets, Yellow-rumped Warblers. Waterfowl and shorebirds continue to come to our beaches, estuaries, and marshes as migrants or winter residents.

*Reprinted from **Sam News**, November 2016*

PHILA ROGERS

New Life and the Old

Three weeks ago we had our first rain. It wasn't much, less than two inches, but it was enough to bring up new grass. Last summer's seeds had lain dormant in the dust until the magical touch of rain signaled it was time to sprout. And what can be more welcome than the vivid green of fresh grass? But beware, unless more rain comes soon, the grass will loose its vitality and the green will fade.

The new grass grows in the open spaces between the stands of dry brush where the winter sparrows feed and sing. The surrounding trees appear exhausted by the years of drought and even the cypress near the edge of the bluff at the Douglas Family Preserve have dropped dead branches and some trees have fallen. The old discarded limbs and the fresh new grass is a tableau of senescence and rebirth. Here on the bluffs above the Pacific Ocean, we see two faces of the natural world.

*Reprinted from **Sam News**, December 2016*

Welcome Winter

The prospects looked poor in November. With a La Nina predicted, meaning the likelihood of a winter with higher than average temperatures and lower than average rainfall, I reconciled myself to the drought continuing. Then December produced a higher-than-average rainfall, and in January after five days of rain, we were two inches above the average for this time of the year (mid-January).

Lawns, which had been brown since last summer, are now radiant green. The same vivid green covers all open spaces, and the ceanothus and manzanitas on the mountain slopes are in bud. Creeks have come to life.

Aside from the deep satisfaction of hearing and smelling the rain itself, the sky was a changing panorama of glorious clouds. And at week's end we were treated to a perfect rainbow whose broad band of color stood out against mountains in shadow.

*Reprinted from **Sam News**, February 2017*

Mobbing Crows — What Are They Up To Anyway?

Though I try my best to ignore them, these big, glossy-black birds with their raucous voices insist on dominating the scene. The most numerous bird species here at Samarkand and around town, crows are here to stay.

That they are so numerous is our fault. Crows rarely live more than five miles away from us. As omnivores, and not fussy eaters, they love our garbage.

Even the more oblivious among us, want to know what's going on when crows stream in from all directions and direct their attention to a certain tree, screaming alerts and diving into its foliage. The behavior is known as mobbing, and the gregarious crows love to join the fun. If you could part the leaves, you are apt to finding an owl or a hawk. Though predators themselves, crows can remember that raptors sometimes prey on crows.

*Reprinted from **Sam News**, February 2017*

The January debris flow in Montecito

Enigma

December beach days. Hibiscus blooming in January. Today, January 29, is supposed to be 80 degrees. But last week, the pre-dawn freeze collapsed the banana leaves in the garden.

Ocean breezes cool most summer days. But at the end of the day, "Sundowners" (our version of Santa Anas) may roar down the mountain canyons from the northeast, elevating the temperature 30 degrees, while lowering the humidity to the single digits.

The sandstone mountains that rise to almost 4,000 feet behind the town, bloom white and then blue in the early spring, releasing a delicate, sweet fragrance. By the end of summer, the chaparral, now dry, can burst into flame and in the presence of a "sundowner" may become a holocaust, threatening the town itself.

Last summer on a hot and humid day, people set up their umbrellas on the beach, or took to the water in small boats. Without warning, one of nature's oddities, a microburst , dropped from the clouds with sheets of rain and hurricane-force winds, capsizing boats, lifting umbrellas into the sky. People dashed for cover.

What is it about Santa Barbara? Why these excesses? Is it that the coast itself defies convention, facing south to the ocean instead of west, and the mountains that run east and west instead of north and south like most of California's mountains? Santa Barbara's ocean is a channel where the winds coming off Point Conception are compressed between the mainland and the string of offshore islands to create some of the roughest seas anywhere.

In October, we begin to wait for the rains which we desperately need in this warming world. November no rain, December no rain. Instead we had the Thomas fire, beginning in the mountains southeast of Ventura, burning for weeks until it reached Montecito where it incinerated the chaparral on the steep mountain slopes. The smoke rained toxic ash and for ten days we had to wear masks.

In the early morning hours of January 9 the rains come, not the gentle rains that bring green grass and wildflowers, but in a torrential, 200-year storm where in five minutes a half-inch rain falls. The water sheets off the burned slopes into the boulder and debris-filled canyons. Within five minutes come the debris flows traveling at 20 miles an hour, carrying boulders some as big as cars, and bodies of those swept from their homes. It was an unspeakable tragedy. My family, though with a home to return to, will be weeks digging out from the hardening mud.

The problem is that Santa Barbara promises so much — physical beauty, and a perfect climate without extremes. But beware — Santa Barbara always has some nasty surprises up its sleeve.

*Reprinted from **Sam News**, February 2018*

Left to Right: Jacaranda tree blossoms, Western Tanager

The Color Purple

Late spring is the season when Santa Barbara turns purple. Along the streets and in the local gardens, Jacaranda trees begin blooming. A native of Brazil, the species adapts well to our semi-tropical climate. Though drought-tolerant, some trees appear to be stressed by our present extreme drought. The trumpet-shaped, blue-purple flowers are carried in profuse 8-inch-long clusters bloom. As the flowers drop, they retain their color, making pools of purple wherever they fall.

Not to be outdone by the jacarandas, agapanthus come on strong this time of the year, both along street planting strips and in gardens. The South-African native produces similar trumpet-shaped flowers but in spherical clusters atop a bare stem. Agapanthus have been hybridized so they come in both standard-sized plants as well as dwarf forms in several shades of blue-purple, along with white varieties.

It appears that May has been generous with some late showers, thanks in part to the jet stream (which delivers our storms) having shifted south. The showers have come with unseasonably cold weather, and even with some short-lived snow falling in the higher elevations.

But with June comes an increase of our coastal fogs. Locals like to refer to this weather as "June Gloom."

And that brilliant, robin-sized yellow bird with black and white wings and an orange-red face that you may catch a glimpse of? It's a male Western Tanager passing through Santa Barbara from its winter home in Mexico to where it may breed in the Sierra Nevada.

*Reprinted from **Sam News**, June 2015*

Left to right: Hooded Oriole. Two male finches (the smaller yellow bird is the Lesser Goldfinch and the larger bird with the red face is the House Finch). Both finches are year-round residents.

Spring Songs

As I write this on March 11, rain is falling accompanied by a gusty wind. The wind shifting abruptly to the west, releases a short-lived torrent of rain. But with no further rain predicted for the near future, we are probably not going to have another "Miracle March" which would have put a dent in our four-year drought.

But no matter, the birds of spring and summer have begun to arrive and the local birds, like the finches, are announcing territories with their songs. Right on schedule, the brilliant Hooded Oriole has arrived from Central America and South America and is feeding on local hummingbird feeders. Other summer residents are soon to follow.

*Reprinted from **Sam News**, Apri 2016*

LEFT TO RIGHT: ELIZABETH COLLINS, CAROL BORNSTEIN

*Left to right:
Blue ceonothus,
Ceonothus
macrocarpus. Photo
courtesy of the Santa
Barbara Botanic
Garden*

The Mountains In Bloom

From the distance the bloom is subtle — maybe like a light snow lying across the brush on the mountainside above. Get up close, and you see that it is clusters of white flowers — the Bigpod Ceanothus. The flowers appear as early as late February.

Within a few weeks the second ceanothus blooms, the Greenbark Ceanothus, this time with pale blue flowers, subtly fragrant. Then the winter rains end, and the time when chaparral plants grow, bloom and set flowers and fruits is over. For the remaining eight months of the year, chaparral endures heat and little moisture, holding on to the steep slopes with their deep roots. Chaparral is superbly adapted to our terrain and climate, growing only in a few other places in the world with similar Mediterranean climates.

To see these remarkable plants close up, visit the Santa Barbara Botanic Garden in Mission Canyon. Most of the planted chaparral grows on the ridge across from the main entrance. Above you are the Santa Ynez Mountains where the chaparral naturally makes its home.

*Reprinted from **Sam News**, March 2017*

(LEFT TO RIGHT): PHILA ROGERS, ROBERT MULLER

Above, left to right: California poppies, distant poppies on Figueroa Mountain. Photo courtesy of the Santa Barbara Botanic Garden

April Flowers At Figueroa Mountain

One of the images I like to conjure up as I'm falling asleep, is the wildflowers of Figueroa Mountain on a spring day. The mountain rises slightly above 4500' on the far edge of the Santa Ynez Valley. The name harks back to Joseph Figueroa, a governor of Alta California before California became a state.

The road up the mountain is narrow and winding. When you find a place to park, leave your car behind so you can look at the flowers close up.

A succession of flowers throughout April should be especially beautiful this year after the bountiful rains.

*Reprinted from **Sam News**, April 2017*

The Color Yellow

Those lovely wildflowers of March and April are fading as grasslands begin to turn from green to gold.

Enter black mustard (Brassica nigra), an import from the Old World, which grows almost everywhere in California except in the high mountains. One theory — a sentimental one — is that the Mission padres scattered seeds to mark the route of the trail between the Missions. More likely, the seeds found their way in the fur of the imported cattle or in cargo.

The warm. bright carpet of mustard bridges the season of green hills of spring wildflowers and the dry heat of summer. Mustard planted in a vineyard as a cover crop both improves the soil structure, adds nitrogen, and discourages nematodes.

In this remarkable year, spring wildflowers of every imaginable kind painted the dry inland hillsides east of San Luis Obispo. By May, the flowers will disappear leaving behind their seeds for another year.

*Reprinted from **Sam News**, May 2017*

PHILA ROGERS

Grass

Since the disastrous deluge of January 9th which destroyed or damaged hundreds of homes in Montecito and took 23 lives, no rain has fallen. That first rainstorm had brought up a fresh winter crop of green grass, but now the blades are growing limp and the color is fading.

Then a welcome storm arrived on March 20. Rain fell for three days in measured amounts, bringing 3 inches of rain but with no further floods or debris flows.

No plant community celebrates the gift of rain more than the grasslands. Almost overnight, bright green grass carpets fields and hillsides.

It appeared that we were being given a second springtime, all the more beautiful for its delayed appearance. For a few weeks, the blades will continue to lengthen. But because most of the grass is composed of annual wild oats, by May the green will turn to gold, ushering in the new season.

*Reprinted from **Sam News**, March 28, 2018*

ANN ALLEN

PHILA ROGERS

Our Special Climate

We are always boasting about the perfection of our climate. But how many of us know that it is indeed special because it only occurs in five places in the world — on the west sides of five continents between the latitudes of 30-40 degrees north and south, and certain areas around the Mediterranean basin. Together these areas make up only 2% of the earth's surface. In addition to the Mediterranean, which gives our climate its name, those regions are the Cape Town region of South Africa, central Chile in South America, California, and parts of the south and west coasts of Australia.

The Mediterranean climate is distinguished by wet, mild winters and long dry, warm (or hot) summers. Sound familiar? One exception is San Francisco with its cool, often cold, foggy summers. But the typically warm/hot summer climates place certain demands on plants that they be hardy enough to withstand months of dryness. The plants need long roots to probe for water and tough, often waxy leaves, to withstand the long days of sunlight. Hence the rugged shrub-lands we call chaparral. I thought the name chaparral came from chaps, the leather leg protection that cowboys wore to spare their legs when they are forced to ride through the almost impassable thickets. But with further research, I discover that chaparral comes from the Spanish word for the scrub oak called chaparro, which is a member of most of the chaparral plant communities.

Each region has their own names for their shrub-lands — garrique around the Mediterranean basin, matorral in Chile, fynbos in South Africa, and kwongan in Australia. All regions have their aromatic plants, like the sages.

Because the regions are widely separated, they each have their distinctive species. We have our manzanitas and ceanothus, but all the plant species share their adaptability to this special climate. Grasslands also adapt to the Mediterranean climate by sprouting new grass, lush and green, in the rainy season, and turning gold (or brown) when the rains stop. As the grass ripens, seeds are released which lay dormant until the rain of the new season awakens them.

Our special climate is vulnerable to climate change which is bringing more severe droughts, more frequent forest fires, and intense winter storms with floods and mudslides. Sound familiar?

Reprinted from **Sam News**, *May 2018*

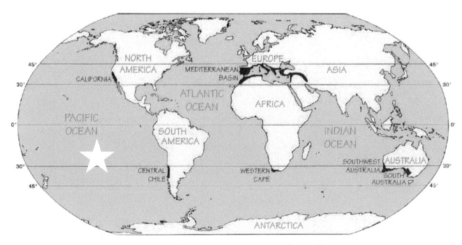

Mediterranean climates (in red)

Somnolent Summer

Except for the brief interruption last month when the remnants of Hurricane Dolores edged north bringing humidity and thunderstorms, it's been the same old summer fog/sun pattern. Summer in coastal California is mostly a long, uneventful pause in the calendar year. But some afternoons, heaping piles of summer cumulus appear above the Santa Ynez Mountains. These are dry clouds and as the air cools in the late afternoon, they disappear.

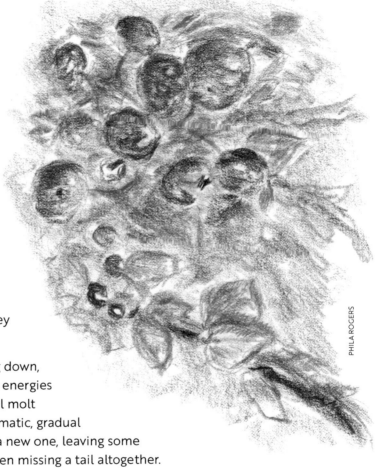

PHILA ROGERS

With breeding season winding down, birds mostly stop singing. Bird energies are now devoted to the annual molt where every feather in a systematic, gradual process must be replaced by a new one, leaving some birds looking disheveled or even missing a tail altogether.

The days are still long and if you choose to, you can match your own rhythm to nature's rhythm by going to bed at sundown and getting up at dawn. But by the end of the month, the days will be growing noticeably shorter. The changing day length is the trigger for bird migration to begin and for flowers to give way to ripening fruit.

While land birds are quiet, with little change in their populations, the shorebirds are beginning to show up after their brief breeding season in the far north. Look along the shore for wheeling flocks of tiny sandpipers or for one of the big wading birds like the Long-billed Curlew.

*Reprinted from **Sam News**, August 2015*

Wild Blooms In Summer Along Camino Cielo

Yucca in Bloom

PHILA ROGERS

The spring wildflowers such as the poppies, lilies, and lupines which had dazzled us in March and April have mostly retreated underground to seed and bulb. So we were surprised to find so many plants in bloom this late in the year along the high ridges of the Santa Ynez Mountains, ranging in colors from brazen reds, purples, and golds.

But the most stunning (and stately) of all are the yuccas (Hesperoyucca whipplei), growing both singly and in groups. The tall yuccas provide an exclamation point to any chaparral-covered slope.

From the center of a roseate of sword-like leaves with razor edges and lethal points, a stalk pushes up like an oversized asparagus to ten feet, culminating in a column of dense, cream-colored flowers, often edged in purple. The tower of flowers seems to glow from within inspiring the common name, Our Lord's Candle.

The sole pollinator is the tiny yucca moth. The plant and the moth have evolved to become dependent on one another for survival. The female moth rolls pollen into a ball, stuffs it into the style (the exposed part of the ovary) of another plant, guaranteeing pollination. She then inserts a few eggs into the ovary ensuring a snack of seeds for her emerging larvae.

Once finished blooming, the drying stalk makes it own architectural statement. And from another roseate of leaves another stalk of flowers will emerge next spring.

*Reprinted from **Sam News**, July 2016*

Looking to the shore

During the summer doldrums when the land birds are quiet, the real action is along the shoreline where the shorebirds have begun their migration. The smallest of all, the sandpipers ("peeps"), true long- distance migrants have finished breeding in the high Arctic and can now be found on the beaches around the world. Though Santa Barbara is deficient in the mud flats, most favored as feeding grounds for shorebirds, our long stretches of sandy beaches are visited by sandpiper flocks who chase waves in and out, stopping only to probe damp sand for tiny marine creatures with their sensitive bills.

What can be more pleasing than seeing a flock take to the air wheeling in unison, exposing first white bellies and then turning to reveal brown backs — a likely scene from an Escher drawing — but in fact a clever way to confuse a predator.

Reprinted from **Sam News**, *August 2016*

BOB LEWIS

Top to bottom: Sandpipers in flight, Sandpiper

PHILA ROGERS

Off With the Old

"My" eucalyptus is shedding. Don't you wish you could shed your old skin (though it's a dematologist's dream) and present a new face to the breezes of summer! I tell my grandchildren I call it the snake tree, though I'm not sure the bark is shed to allow room for new growth. In fact, most trees shed their bark because its old and often diseased.

Of all the "eucs" this one (Eucalyptus citriodora) with its sinuous, white limbs and long, slender leaves must be the pride of the family. Eucs have been here for such a long time — since the mid-nineteenth century — most people think they are a native, but most eucalyptus are a native of Australia. Crush some of its leaves so you can inhale the delicious, citrusy smell, and you'll understand why it contributes to so many products.

*Reprinted from **Sam News**, June 2017*

THE END OF SUMMER

Crickets singing in the last long evenings,
Daylight coming later,
First Redbud leaves turning gold,
Monarchs drifting over gardens -
Signs of the approach of fall.

Summer heat may continue into November
Ahead of the first rains and cold nights

Over the restless Pacific,
The bringer of our weather,
The high pressure is moving south
Opening the storm door,
Taming the summer winds
That brought fog and cold seas.

Warm water now has come to the coast
Helped by a building El Nino,
Bringing hard times
To sea birds and animals of the sea
As small prey fish move north
In search of colder waters.

The sun begins its slow journey
Into the southern skies,
Its winter home,
When the fall equinox marks
A night and day of equal length.

While September may be the month
Of a slow indrawn breath,
The month of waiting is over
October, the joyous month, brings
The arrival of the winter birds
And sparrow songs to fill our gardens.

*Reprinted from **Sam News**, September 2018*

HANNO LEWIS

Birdwatching at Almost Ninety

I was out on a jaunt with my Berkeley friends, Hanno and Bob Lewis, to a posted 'hot spot' in Winchester Canyon. Beyond the lawn is a group of rather anemic-looking eucalyptus trees being disfigured by a heavy infestation of a small sucking insects called physslids. With their protective covers they are called lerps, and they are catnip to warblers and other small birds.

We saw a number of warblers in the trees, but we missed the rarities. No matter. As usual we were enjoying ourselves — Bob, rarely without his camera (see his website "bob@wingbeats.org" for his global birds) and Hanno, his travelling companion, who has an eye for the telling shots.

HUCK RANSON

Left to right:
Blue-Winged
Warbler, Ovenbird

Two birds stand out in this migratory season. I had missed both. I didn't take missing the Ovenbird lightly as I truly yearned to see this "Ground-walking Warbler" with its tail often held high like a wren's, a thrush-like streaked and spotted breast, and splayed toes for shuffling through fallen leaves. The Ovenbird takes its name from its unusual nest.

A late migrator, the Blue-winged Warbler, was the first sighting ever in Santa Barbara county. A true beauty, it was seen for a few days in the Carpinteria creek bed. But with its steep slopes, it was accessible only to the sure-footed.

With most migrants now on their wintering grounds, I listen for our winter residents, especially the "chuck chucks' of the Hermit Thrush whom I associate with winter rains.

*Reprinted from **Sam News***

Mission Creek

Of all the forms water can take
It's the creek which pleases me most.
The ocean is too vast and where it meets
Our shore too rambunctious.
Reservoirs feel confined.
Lakes, though serving as reflective mirrors,
Are too far away.

PHILA ROGERS

My creek begins its life as springs
Hidden by rock and chaparral
below La Cumbre Peak
Where it starts its long journey
down the mountains slopes,
To meander across the sloping plain,
Before it enters the sea.

With the heavy rains of February
The creek was a torrent of tan water
Clawing at its banks, hungry for release.

After several days of sun,
The water has cleared
The loud gnashing of rocks
is now a soft murmur of riffles.
Or where in the lee of a boulder,
the moving water may form pools
reflecting the pale trunks of a sycamore.

Yesterday, I walked along it banks
Pacing my stride to match its flow
I imagined the creek flowing through my
Veins and I was refreshed.

I will try not to grieve when the creek dries up
At the end of the rainy season.
After all, this is an ephemeral stream
Destined to retire underground,
Where, safely stored, roots can find it.

In this winter of generous rains
That may have ended the drought
Let's rejoice!

Acknowledgements

George Dumas, my webmaster, who made it happen.

Roger Bradfield, a dear friend, who was then living at The Samarkand. He is the author and illustrator of many childrens' books. He drew the sketches for some of my essays.

Nancy Law, my daughter, editor, honest critic, and cheerleader.

Stuart Law, my grandson who saved me from many a computer disaster. Together, we put on "power point" shows at Samarkand about local birds.

Tom Ginn, photographer living here at Samarkand who is responsible for so many of the splendid photographs.

Bob Lewis, another fine photographer and bird expert, a dear friend from the Berkeley days.

Helen Bernson, an administrator here at Samarkand who puts together Sam News, the in-house monthly publication — another cheerleader.

Joan Lentz, birder extraordinaire and inspirer, author of "A Naturalist' Guide to the Santa Barbara Region" who let me use some of the drawings.

Dr. Stanley McLain who helped keep me together this long.

Karin Shelton, whose beautiful cover painting made the book something special.

Ann Allen, my partner in Samarkand's Native Plant Garden and a watercolor painter of native plants, whose drawings of a Douglas Iris and Mariposa Lily are on page 122.

THE BIRDS HAVE VANISHED

BY LI PO 701-762

The birds have vanished into the sky,

And now the last cloud drains away.

We sit together, the mountain and me,

Until only the mountain remains.

About the Author

Clipping sage in the Samarkand native plant garden.

Birdwatcher and naturalist, Phila Rogers has been living full time in Santa Barbara for the last seven years, having moved from her house in the Berkeley hills where she had lived for 63 years. She lives in a retirement community, located next to Oak Park and Mission Creek where she is learning a new place with mountains instead of hills, an ocean close by instead of the shores of San Francisco Bay. This book is the result of seven years of close observation.

In the Bay Area, she wrote a number of articles and essays and with her husband, Don Witherell, wrote a weekly nature column for the Oakland Tribune. With her daughter, Nancy Law, she wrote and produced *California Tales: From the Mountains to the Sea*.

Made in the USA
Lexington, KY
06 December 2019